AN ILLUSTRATED HISTORY OF THE
HAUNTED WORLD

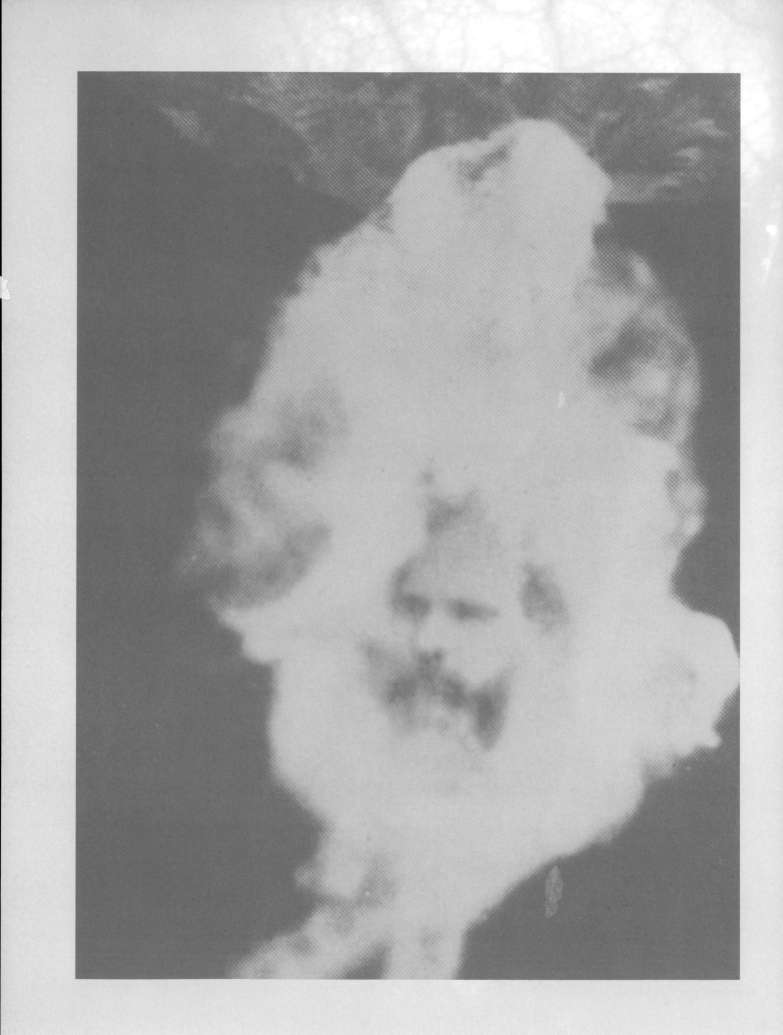

AN ILLUSTRATED HISTORY OF THE
HAUNTED WORLD

JASON KARL

NEW HOLLAND

First published in 2007 by New Holland Publishers (UK) Ltd
London • Cape Town • Sydney • Auckland
www.newhollandpublishers.com

Garfield House, 86–88 Edgware Road,
London W2 2EA, United Kingdom

80 McKenzie Street, Cape Town 8001,
South Africa

Unit 1, 66 Gibbes Street, Chatswood,
NSW 2067, Australia

218 Lake Road, Northcote, Auckland,
New Zealand

10 9 8 7 6 5 4 3 2 1

ISBN 978 1 84537 6871

Publishing Manager: Jo Hemmings
Project Editors: Gareth Jones, Steffanie Brown, Naomi Waters
Editor: Simon Pooley
Designer: Gülen Shevki-Taylor
Production: Joan Woodroffe

Reproduction by Pica Digital PTE Ltd, Singapore
Printed and bound in Singapore by Star Standrad

DEDICATION
This book is dedicated to the world's leading ghost hunters past and
present, and to my grandmother 'Dee' for all her loving support in
my ghostly endeavours!

Front cover: A modern-day witch looks into the haunted world.
Back cover: A spectre, table-tilting and spirit celebration.
Front flap: A glowing jack-o-lantern frightens away spooks at
Samhain.
Page 2: A phantom face emerges from ectoplasm.
Half-title page: An artist's impression of a trial at Salem,
Massachusetts.
Title page: A depiction of ghosts atop a levitating piano.
Opposite: A candlestick is thrown through the air by an unseen but
powerful force.
Page 6: A photographer's depiction of a haunted staircase.

CONTENTS

Foreword

Having been involved with serious, objective, scientific research into the strange, the anomalous and the unsolved for more than 40 years, it is a great pleasure to come across a superbly organized and expertly written new book on the subject.

Jason begins with a methodical survey of famous hauntings through the ages up to our current preoccupation with hidden cameras and media ghosts. Cases in his exciting and intriguing opening chapter raise the fascinating question of the extent to which poltergeist phenomena and some allied manifestations are dependent upon the minds of the observers. With 1014 neurones in the average human brain, and with a single, identifiable thought defined as an electro-chemical track between any two (or more!) neurones, our brains are theoretically capable of thinking as many thoughts as there are atoms in the universe – which is as near to infinity as matters in both cases.

To understate the case dramatically – the human brain is an exceptionally powerful mechanism, only a small percentage of which is currently understood and used. If teleportation, telekinesis and telepathy really exist – and there is a weight of evidence for them – then it is arguable that the human *mind* has powers beyond our current imaginings: such a potent entity is unlikely to succumb just because its physical launching pad (the biological *brain*) has ceased to exist.

Among the world-famous cases that Jason analyses so well is the Amherst Poltergeist in Nova Scotia, an inexplicable phenomenon that tormented 19-year-old Esther Cox in 1878. One of the factors that make this book so readable is the careful selection of notorious cases like this one, set alongside several new and little-known accounts.

In his second chapter, Jason pays close attention to festivals concerned with the dead, placating and honouring the spirits of ancestors and forebears – his accounts range from Germany's Walpurgis Night to Scotland's Belthane, also rendered Beltane. His third chapter looks closely at spirit photographs – another intriguing area of paranormal research. One of the strangest examples that my wife Patricia and I investigated was provided by our friend Simon Probert of Penarth. We had recently completed a BBC documentary on the moving coffins in the Chase Elliot vault, situated in the Christchurch Cemetery, at Oistins, in Barbados. Simon and his friend Pamela Willson had also visited the area and Pam had taken a picture of Simon on the steps of the vault. The rest of their film had developed normally. The picture of the vault was a weird blur *until it was subjected to computer analysis*. What then emerged clearly was a skull surrounded by what the Victorian spiritualists would have described as ectoplasm. Knowing Simon and Pamela as we do, and vouching 100 per cent for their integrity and the genuineness of their picture of the Chase Elliot vault, Patricia and I are intrigued by that picture – and by spirit photographs in general. It seems as though the camera can occasionally pick up what the eye fails to see – just as there are occasions on which the eye seems to record what the camera doesn't.

Jason's fourth chapter investigates the various methods that have been used by mediums, séance groups and investigators over the years in the hope of communicating with the spirits of the dead. Scrying techniques, Ouija boards, table tilting and automatic writing all come under scrutiny. He also looks into mediumship. My wife and I have worked with some gifted and abnormally perceptive individuals, who are able to contact those who have left this world.

Famous personalities associated with the paranormal form the subject of Chapter Five, and include Nostradamus. I presented the TV documentary *The Real Nostradamus* for Channel 4

in 1999, and was a contributor to *Nostradamus: the truth* on the Discovery Channel in 2006. During the course of filming the latter programme in the Church of St Laurent in Salon, Provence, France, where Nostradamus is buried in the wall, an automatic light high above the film crew's heads was focussed on Nostradamus's white marble memorial slab against which we were trying to film my piece to camera. That light suddenly went stroboscopic so that we were unable to work.

'I can compensate if it's off; and I can work with it on', said our cameraman, 'but I can't film against that strobe!' We tried pulling out every plug we could find in the church, to no avail. The light went strobing on! My cameraman friend said suddenly: 'Lionel, you're a priest, do you think it's Nostradamus mucking us about? Could you say a prayer for him, or something?'

I didn't think for a moment that it was the restless spirit of Nostradamus having fun at our expense, but I went along with the request for prayer, and duly blessed Nostradamus and his tomb. As I said 'Amen' the light went out and stayed out, and, thankfully, we completed our film. It could well have been mere coincidence, but there *might* have been a psychic explanation.

Jason's final chapter looks into modern, scientific investigative techniques of researching the paranormal and the anomalous. All in all, this book is a very important and worthwhile addition to any library of the paranormal – as a professional investigator and researcher, I am more than happy to have this opportunity of recommending Jason's excellent work.

LIONEL FANTHORPE
President of the Association for the Scientific Study of Anomalous Phenomena

Introduction

OUR WORLD IS HAUNTED

Around every corner lies the unseen world, just out of our grasp, just in the next room...

Since the dawn of time we humans have believed in forces greater than ourselves. Historians have traced the development of religion back to the Neolithic period of the 10th millennium BC, where cave paintings told stories of the Mother Goddess, represented as the moon, and the Father of the Sky, represented by the sun. Belief in the divine powers of the forces we see around us is commonplace even today in belief systems such as Wicca and Paganism. Belief in the supernatural in some form or other is fundamental to all religions.

It is easier to go through life believing that there is 'something' out there. Perhaps it is a kind of insurance policy for the afterlife? Despite living in a scientifically oriented world we still cling to the beliefs which our ancestors never questioned; as a species, we need hope – and hope comes in many guises.

Have you ever seen a ghost? Felt a cold chill which was unexplained, or glimpsed something out of the corner of your eye which you are sure had a humanoid shape? The belief that we exist beyond physical life is as old as history itself, with practically all religious faith systems incorporating the acceptance that our body and soul part at the time of death, and the soul continues in some capacity. These 'ghosts' can, it is said, return to the land where they once walked, often in response to a ritual performed by their living counterparts, or at a special time of the year when the conditions are right.

The evidence presented to the scientific world is ever increasing and many scholars of quantum physics are now looking at potential ways of exploring alternative realities that might exist, and of which we are, for the most part, blissfully unaware. There are photographs from the Victorian era purportedly depicting the spirits of the dead, posing perfectly for the camera – but these would not stand up to modern techniques of analysis. But what of the famous 'Ghost of Raynham Hall' – science has yet to disprove that she was floating down the staircase during the visit of two photographers in 1936. And what of the plethora of other ghostly evidence caught on video, and the voices in empty rooms caught on sound recorders? Science has previously sought to disprove the existence of supernatural phenomena, but now our technology is not disproving the existence of the haunted world, it is helping us to find new ways of experiencing it.

Having undertaken to trawl through the history of the haunted world I have come across experiences which have touched people from every walk of life, in all corners of the globe and throughout all time periods. These encounters are not confined to one part of the world or to a certain type of 'psychic' person – in many cases quite the opposite. Anyone, anywhere, at any time, might find themselves crossing over to an alternative world and experiencing something of the supernatural. But we have no reason to fear the haunted realm. It is part of us, just as one day we might become part of it.

Here then is my history of the haunted world, a journey through time into the haunted past and present. I have been selective in presenting a variety of cases, stories and evidence which have arisen since the beginning of recorded history, with a bias towards those of a spectral nature. As you might expect with a book chronicling ghostly history since the dawn of time, there is far too much data to present everything available, and therefore each entry gives a general view of that period of haunted history.

I have presented the 'facts' as I have found them, recorded from a variety of printed sources. I make no guarantee that the stories included actually happened, merely that there are records which state that they did. It is up to the reader to remain objective and make his or her own mind up about what to believe. Belief is a personal thing and for those whose lives have not been touched by the other side, some of the contents may be hard to accept as real. What I can say is that the people to whom they occurred believed entirely in an unseen world beyond our usual realm of understanding.

As the clock ticks ever forward and the world becomes ever smaller, the global shift towards a New Age consciousness will uncover more remarkable encounters with the haunted world. If you have a page of your own paranormal history to add to this collection please do get in touch via my website below, but for now, enjoy this delve into the shadow realms, as I uncover the history of the haunted world.

Jason Dexter Karl
www.jasondexterkarl.com

Chapter 1
A History of Hauntings

Stories about ghosts, spirits and phantasms have intrigued us from time immemorial. But what of the real haunted houses, the real ghost stories and the real reactions people have to coping with unwanted visitors from another world?

In this chapter I will take you on a whistle-stop tour of the most infamous cases where the haunted world has come into the lives of the living. We will visit the famous Epworth Rectory, where a classic poltergeist caused havoc for Samuel Wesley, father of John Wesley and an early Methodist leader. We will see how fear of witchcraft lead to the death of 10 innocent people at Pendle Hill in the 17th century, and we will hear the tragedy of the witches of Salem in America. We will meet a man who claims that his computer communicated with the ghost of a man who had lived in his house hundreds of years earlier and hear the incredible tale of the cursed Hexham Heads, which brought a peculiar 'wolf-like' haunting into the home of an otherwise tranquil family.

How has Hollywood embroidered the stories we see on the big screen in films such as *The Exorcist* and *The Amityville Horror*? Do the records of the real incidents match up to what is seen on screen? We will examine the cases dramatised by the screenwriters and find that the truth is, in some cases, more frightening than the films.

What of Borley Rectory, the most haunted house in Britain? A modern-day 'Mecca' for ghost hunters, this once-famous house burned down under strange circumstance in 1939 – and it still produces psychic phenomena today. Is the evidence strong, or is this a vain attempt to keep alive a ghost story that was buried many years ago?

As science tries to disprove what many believe and countless have experienced, we will examine the evidence in each case and look at the incidents with a fresh eye. Are these tales merely the product of wild imaginations and conveniently pieced together histories? Or are they reliable accounts of a real phenomenon which shows itself only to the very lucky, or unlucky, few?

THE PENDLE WITCHES
18 March–20 August 1612

It was on 18 March 1612, that Alizon Device – on her way to the village of Trawden to beg for money – came across a traveller named John Law, walking from Halifax. The two met on a road near Colne on the edge of the Forest of Pendle in Lancashire. This meeting was to spell the beginning of the most famous case of witchcraft in the history of Britain – the tale of the Pendle Witches.

Angered when John Law ignored her request for some pins from the pack on his back, Alizon shrieked a curse on him, at which point he fell immediately to the ground in a seizure, foaming at the mouth, an image of a black dog with fiery eyes filling his mind before he blacked out. He was taken to a local tavern where his son, Abraham, was summoned to tend to his father. When asked what had occurred, John answered that he had met with a beggar-woman on the track who had cursed him with her hellhound. From his description they easily recognised her as the granddaughter of the hated 'Demdike', a wizened crone believed to be a witch who lived with Alizon and the rest of her family in Malkin Tower near Lower Well Head Farm. Alizon was summoned to the bed of John Law to explain herself. Filled with remorse, and apparently believing that she had indeed conjured some power from Hell, she begged forgiveness for cursing him. But Abraham had already involved the long arm of the law, and he took her to Read Hall where, on 30 March, she stood before Magistrate Roger Nowell to answer the charge of witchcraft.

PREVIOUS PAGE: *A haunted figure emerges in an allegedly haunted chamber.*

BELOW: *Pendle Hill is a notorious site for sightings of ghosts and witches.*

Accompanied by her mother Elizabeth, a deformed widow, and her mentally challenged brother James Device, she confessed under interrogation that she was a witch, and that the hellhound seen by John Law was her evil familiar. Alizon added that she had been taught the ways of a witch by her grandmother 'Demdike' (whose real name was Elizabeth Southern), an 80-year-old blind woman feared throughout Pendle for her ugly appearance and spiteful manner. Alizon alleged that her entire family were witches, ensuring that they too would be examined by Nowell.

After Alizon was confined, Roger Nowell continued his investigation into the claims of witchcraft in Pendle, this time at Ashlar House in Fence. On 2 April, Demdike herself confessed that she was in league with the Devil who, she claimed under interrogation, had first appeared to her at Newchurch in Pendle in the form of a young boy named 'Tibb', who transformed into a dog and sucked the blood from her shrivelling body. Demdike also claimed that Tibb had aided her in the murder of a child of Richard Baldwin of Wheathead – who owed her family money at the time.

Why these wild confessions were so freely given remains a mystery to this day. Despite being interrogated by a respected magistrate, Demdike and her family could quite easily have claimed their innocence for they were under no duress to confess and no tortures where used to extract confessions of witchery. Had they remained silent there would very probably have been no trial and no executions. It is speculated that confessions were given in the hope of receiving mercy, but if that was the case they were to be sorely disappointed…

The arch enemies of the Device family lived in a dirty hovel at nearby Greenhead. Led by their grandmother Anne Whittle, known locally as 'Chattox' after her maiden name of Chadwick, the family was poor and as detested locally as was Demdike's. They became embroiled in the saga at the outset because Demdike and Chattox, who had once been friends, had become bitter enemies. In an attempt to incriminate Demdike further, Chattox told Nowell that she had been initiated into witchcraft 14 years earlier by Demdike. She also confessed that she, like her rival, had a familiar (hers was named 'Fancie'). By now gossip was spreading across Pendle and more 'witnesses' came forward to give accounts of magical conjurings they had seen. The result was that Demdike, her granddaughter Alizon, Chattox and her daughter Anne Redfearn were sent to Lancaster Castle dungeons to await

ABOVE: *A stone 'eye' stares down into the graveyard at Newchurch-in-Pendle, Lancashire, UK.*

a formal trial, each charged with murder under the Witchcraft Act of 1604.

Talk of dark happenings around the Hill was now commonplace and a few days later wagging tongues resulted in a witches' sabbat being reported to Nowell on Good Friday. This had allegedly taken place at Malkin Tower, where a brood of other witches had plotted to rescue their imprisoned cohorts. Evidence in the shape of clay effigies and human teeth were discovered at the Tower and were accepted as strong enough evidence to justify further investigation. On 27 April, Roger Nowell was joined by fellow magistrate Nicholas Bannister, with whom he questioned the remainder of Demdike's family; her deformed daughter Elizabeth (known locally as 'Squintin' Lizzie'), her granddaughter Jennet and her grandson James. Accusations were thrown at a number of local villagers, including Alice Nutter (from whence the modern derogatory term 'nutter' derives), a respected resident of nearby Roughlee Hall. By the end of the examination a further seven 'witches' were marched off to Lancaster to join those already incarcerated, to await trial. Jennet Preston of Gisburn, whose name had been given to the magistrates as present at the Malkin Tower meeting, was taken to York, faced trial and was hanged on Wednesday 29 July after being found guilty of the murder of one Thomas Lister.

ABOVE: *A Witches' Sabbat, during which spells and potions are brewed.*

On Tuesday 18 August 1612, the assizes were held before Sir Edward Bromley and Sir James Altham, with Roger Nowell continuing his role as prosecutor for the court. Anne Whittle was first to face the judges. She was accused of using the power of witchcraft to kill Robert Nutter in 1595, a charge she denied but because she had already confessed to the murder, was found guilty. Elizabeth Device was next, facing charges of three counts of murder backed up by the evidence of her own daughter Jennet. She was also found guilty, along with James Device. The next day Anne Redfearn, Alizon Device, Alice Nutter, Katherine Hewitt, John Bulcock, Margaret Pearson of Padiham and Isobel Robey of Windle were all found guilty as charged and sentenced to execution. The judge said 'You shall go hence to the Castle from whence you came, from thence you shall be carried to the place of execution for this county, where your bodies shall be hanging (sic) until dead. And may God have mercy upon your souls'. On Thursday 20 August, cheers rang out around Lancaster as the ten 'witches' were executed, one by one, at Gallows Hill. Demdike was the only one to escape the hangman's rope, as she perished in the dungeon beneath the Well Tower at Lancaster Castle, having succumbed due to her advanced age and the terrible conditions of no sanitation, food or water.

The case of the Pendle witch craze is unique in that a perfect record of the events was recorded by Thomas Potts at the time. The text *The Wunderfull Discoverie of Witches in the Countie of Lancaster* is still in print and remains the most authoritative source of facts surrounding the incidents of 1612.

Modern scholars and experts analysing the accounts are divided in their opinions as to why the trials were unfairly biased in favour of finding witches and not necessarily the 'truth' of the situations. It has been suggested that the 'witches' were nothing more than innocent dupes, sacrificed by ambitious judges to find favour with the monarch, James I. The king was a known hater of witches after he attended a trial in 1590 at which several people were convicted of attempting to bewitch a ship upon which he was travelling. He wrote a huge treatise on demonology, sorcery and witchcraft, the result of which was that hundreds of women in Scotland were put to death as witches.

Malkin Tower was demolished shortly after the witch trials but remnants are known to have remained as late as 1900; sadly, nothing of the building now remains. Pendle is still at the centre of the witchcraft community and serves as a place of ritual for many modern-day witches and Pagans, many of whom gather at the hill each Hallowe'en. The local tourist industry relies heavily on the historical association with the paranormal and local tours offer the chance to see the 'haunts of the Pendle Witches'. Businesses such as Witches Galore – the highly popular souvenir shop in Newchurch – are based entirely on the story, capitalizing on a tale which may, or may not, have had a supernatural origin.

BELOW: *A Witches' Ball hangs to deflect evil forces from the home, and is the forefather of the Christmas tree baubles we hang today.*

THE SALEM WITCH HUNT
June–September 1692

From June to September 1692 witchcraft and devilry swept through the otherwise sleepy seaport of Salem, Massachusetts. Mass hysteria, fear and jealousy gripped the townsfolk who threw accusation upon accusation at each other resulting in the deaths of 24 innocent people. A naïve judgement system and a staunch Puritan faith ensured that the hangman's noose on nearby Gallows Hill was rarely empty before the neck of the next victim was thrust within it; and then, just months after it had begun, the now infamous witch hunt was over.

Four years earlier, in 1688, town elder John Putnam invited Samuel Parris, a merchant based in Barbados, to preach in the village church. Twelve months later Parris had moved permanently to Salem with his wife Elizabeth, daughter Betty, niece Abagail Williams and his Indian slave, Tituba. It was the colour of this unfortunate servant's skin and her loose tongue which sowed the seed of the witch hunt that would soon follow.

The story begins one cold winter night in February 1692 when 10-year-old Betty Parris, daughter of village minister Samuel Parris, was struck down by an unknown illness. Her strange convulsions and feverish temperature, which might today be explained as epilepsy or psychosis, were not understood in the rural towns of 17th-century America. Communication with the outside world was limited. Local doctor William Griggs was relied upon to explain Betty's condition; he suggested that the cause of Betty's and subsequently others' behaviour might have a supernatural origin. The timing of this diagnosis spelled doom for many of Salem's residents, as comparisons were quickly drawn between Betty's symptoms and entries in a recently published book which had been widely accepted across America. *Memorable Providences*, by Cotton Mather, described in detail a case of suspected witchcraft possession

BELOW: *A traditional image of a witch atop her besom and accompanied by two black cat familiars.*

of an Irish washerwoman in Boston city; the symptoms exhibited matched closely with Betty's.

Wagging tongues in a small town ensured that talk of the devil in Salem spread like wildfire among the townsfolk and when three further children – 17-year-old Mercy Lewis, 18-year-old Mary Walcott and 11-year-old Ann Putnam – became afflicted, apparently with the same illness, suspicion of witchcraft became firmly rooted in the small-town mentality of Salem.

Tales of voodoo, omens and witchcraft in Tituba's native culture ensured that suspicion fell heavily upon her, and when she was advised by neighbour Mary Sibley to perform a 'counter-spell' by baking a cake of rye and urine and feeding it to a dog, this only added to speculation that she was responsible for the unexplained illnesses. Soon the number of afflicted children had risen to eight, with the addition of Susannah Sheldon, Elizabeth Hubbard, Abagail Williams and Mary Warren. These friends now became a 'gang of juvenile delinquents' according to one historian, and exhibited a variety of frightening postures, grotesque contortions and complained of being bitten and pinched by unseen forces. The belief that this was the devil's work was now widely accepted in Salem, and efforts to find the culprit who had brought evil to the town became an obsession.

On 29 February, Tituba, a beggar-woman named Sarah Good, and bedridden Sarah Osborne were the first in a long line of men, women and children to be arrested under accusation of practising witchcraft. County magistrates Jonathan Corwin and John Hathorne had them locked up, scheduling a trial for the following day, 1 March.

By the morning of the 'witches" examination news of the trial had already travelled far and wide, and hundreds turned up to watch as they were questioned; so many that the trial was moved from a local inn to the nearby Meeting House. Betty, Abagail and the other accusers displayed the same disturbing behaviour which had sown the seed of suspected devilment weeks earlier and described how they had been visited by the witches in spectral form and had been tormented by them – causing their contortions and pains. Although it is apparent that the magistrates clearly thought the women guilty from their style of questioning, this may well have been the end of the saga had it not been for Tituba. Afraid of being used as a scapegoat, she decided to confess that she was indeed a witch and had been visited by a tall man in black whom she believed was Satan himself. She claimed that he had made her sign a pact and carry out his work. She also sealed the fate of Good, Osborne and two others, telling the court that all five of them had flown through the air on their broomsticks. This admission by Tituba silenced the sceptics and guaranteed that a full-scale witch hunt began without delay.

Within weeks, Betty and Abagail testified that the spectral forms of other women were attacking them, and subsequently Mary Eastey, Rebecca Nurse and Martha Corey were formally accused. Next was Ann Putnam who 'saw' a witch's form, this time during a church service on 20 March. She suddenly proclaimed 'Look where Goodwife Cloyce sits on the beam suckling her yellow bird!' All four accused women were thrown in jail to await trial and were joined shortly afterwards by four-year-old Dorcas Good, daughter of Sarah Good. Dorcas was the first child to be accused of witchcraft, after three of the girls reported to the authorities that they had been bitten by her spectre. Tragically, Dorcas was kept in jail for eight months before watching her mother being taken up to Gallows Hill and executed. Meanwhile, news of witchcraft in Salem was spreading across America. The public displays of pain and contorted poises exhibited by the accusers were enhanced by the new symptom of being 'struck dumb'; this occurring only in the presence of the 'witches' that were being accused by the young afflicted.

Confession was the only means of escape for the accused and soon Deliverance Hobbs followed in Tituba's footsteps by confessing that she was a witch, admitting that she had pinched the afflicted under the guidance of Satan and had flown to a field upon a pole to celebrate a witches' sabbat. As the jail approached maximum capacity it was clear that a new form of trial must be instigated, and following the return of Governor Phips from England, a new court was formed to hear each witchcraft case. The panel consisted of five judges led by witch hunter William Stoughton, and included several colleagues of witchcraft author, Cotton Mather.

The new court allowed a strange variety of new evidence to be considered including 'spectral evidence' – the testimony of the afflicted that the spirit of each alleged witch had attacked them. In modern times this would be dismissed as mere hearsay or gossip, but in 17th-century Salem it was accepted as the truth and not questioned. Also allowed was the 'touch test' whereby defendants were requested to touch the afflicted to see if this would cause their symptoms to cease – proving that they must be a witch. Accepted too was the examination of the bodies of those accused in order to find 'witches' marks' believed to be areas where the witch's familiar might suckle. In common terms this meant that any large moles or birthmarks might be accepted as 'evidence' of a union with Satan.

On 2 June, Bridget Bishop was the first to be tried in the new court. As an innkeeper who allowed customers to enjoy a beverage on the Sabbath day she was an easy target for prosecutor Thomas Newton, who was confident of securing a guilty verdict. During the trial a farm worker stated that he had seen her spectre stealing food, and another – a villager by the

BELOW: *A modern depiction of a witch of Salem, a far cry from the wart-ridden hags history has had us believe inhabited Salem village.*

ABOVE: *The grim face of justice still keeps watch over Salem, Massachusetts.*

name of Samuel Grey – announced that Bishop had attacked him in his bed in the dead of night. Examination of her body found that she had the marks of the devil upon her and as the villagers gave testimony against her the rope was being prepared for her departure into the next world. After Justice Stoughton signed her death warrant following a guilty verdict, one of the Judges, Nathaniel Saltonstall, resigned from the court – reportedly horrified at the conduct he had witnessed. Bridget Bishop was hung on Gallows Hill on 10 June 1692.

Throughout a hot summer the witch trials gathered pace. Next to be accused was Rebecca Nurse, a respected pillar of the community accused by Ann Putnam and Abagail Williams of attacking them and trying to get them to sign a pact with the Devil. Nurse was a member of the Topsfield family who had a long-standing dispute with the Putnams, but this incentive for Ann Putnam to testify against Nurse was overlooked. Evidence that Nurse had cursed Benjamin Houlton because his pig had strayed onto her land, and thus caused his death, ensured that she was eventually – having initially been found not-guilty – sentenced to death on 19 July.

The witch craze was now in full swing and those who viewed the accusers with suspicion were themselves at risk of being accused and subsequently tried as witches. John Proctor, an opinionated innkeeper, spoke out against the witch hunt and paid dearly for his attitude – with his life. After being accused of being in league with Lucifer by Ann, Abagail and a slave of Samuel Parris who worked in a competing inn, he was tried and convicted of witchcraft along with his wife, Elizabeth, and sentenced to be executed on Gallows Hill.

By now it was believed that the witches must have a ringleader, a kind of 'soldier of Satan', and the man accused of playing this role was Salem's ex-minister George Burroughs, who had moved from Salem to Maine but was brought back for trial. Burroughs was identified by several of the afflicted and accused by Ann Putnam of bewitching a failed military frontier war effort in 1688. The most vociferous evidence against Burroughs came from the mouth of 19-year-old Mercy Lewis. A refugee of the frontier wars, Mercy described how he had 'flown her to the top of a mountain and, indicating the surrounding lands, promised her the entire kingdom if only she would sign his book'. She testified that she replied 'I would not writ if he had throwed me down on 100 pitchforks'. George Burroughs was convicted and hanged, insisting on his innocence to the last breath and screaming out the Lord's Prayer as the noose was tightened around his Puritan neck.

The madness that had swept through Salem was drawing to a close by early autumn when farmer Giles Corey, who had spent five months in jail with his wife after they had been accused of witchery, was killed. He was not hanged, but pressed under stones until his body was crushed from the weight expunging his final breath. Seeing the futility of the trials and possessing a canny knowledge of the law, he knew that if he refused a trial and thus a possible conviction his land would not be granted to the State, but rather to his two sons-in-law. The penalty for refusing trial was *Peine Forte et Dure* – or death by pressing. Defiant to the end, his final words are laced with tragic humour and are recorded as 'put on more weight'. Three days later on 22 September 1692, Giles' wife Martha and seven other 'witches' were the last to be hanged in Salem. At last, the witch hunt was over.

Doubts had been developing in the minds of Salem's educated elite for some time. Reverend John Hale said, 'It cannot be imagined that in a place of so much knowledge, so many in so small compass of land should abominably leap into the Devil's lap at once'. The hysteria which had enveloped Salem for so many months was waning. The publication of *Cases of Conscience* by Increase Mather (father of Cotton) further dissipated the witch obsession, arguing that 'it is better that 10 suspected witches should escape than one innocent person should be condemned'. The author advised the court that speculative forms of testimony should be excluded from trials and subsequently 'spectral evidence', the 'touch test' and seeking the marks of Satan on the bodies of the accused were abolished. With no other forms of solid evidence available, 28 of the last 33 trials resulted in acquittals, and those who were convicted under the 'new rules' that followed were later pardoned. In May 1693, the remaining accused and convicted who had been held in jail over the winter, were released without charge.

By the end of the Salem witch hunt 19 convicted witches had lost their lives on Gallows Hill. They were: Bridget Bishop, Rebecca Nurse, Sarah Good, Susannah Martin, Elizabeth Howe, Sarah Wildes, George Burroughs, Martha Carrier, John Willard, George Jacobs, John Proctor, Martha Corey, Mary Eastey, Ann Pudeator, Alice Parker, Mary Parker, Wilmott Redd, Margaret Scott and Samuel Wardwell. Giles Corey had been pressed to death after refusing trial, and 17 other convicted 'witches' died in jail. Two dogs were also put to death after they had been found to be 'witches' familiars'.

In all, 37 people lost their lives, and a further 200 suffered at the hands of a questionable legal system and a town filled with fear, hatred, jealousy and puritanical obsession. The 'witches' of Salem were nothing more than innocent townsfolk who got caught up in a madness fuelled by naivety. Their story must be remembered, along with the lessons learned from these events, for generations to come.

BELOW: *The infamous 'witch house' is now a popular tourist attraction.*

THE POLTERGEIST OF EPWORTH RECTORY

1 December 1716–31 January 1717

It was the servants who first heard the sounds of a dying man by the dining room door at 10pm on 1 December 1716. Manservant Robert Brown and a housemaid assumed that it was the final groans of neighbour Mr Turpine who had been ill for some time and had occasionally visited the rectory. But when they opened the door there was nothing to account for the sounds they had heard. The moment they closed the door once more, loud agitated rappings began to emanate from the wood. Robert opened the door swiftly, at which point the deafening knockings immediately ceased, leaving the pair staring blankly into the hallway with no apparent explanation for what they had heard. Perplexed by the encounter they bid each other goodnight and made their separate ways to bed, but for Robert, his night with the unexplained was young. As he crept quietly through the house and ascended the steps to his bedchamber high in the garret, he was stopped in his tracks midway, for at the top of the stairs a hand mill was moving at great speed – of its own volition. Later, as he lay in bed trying to sleep, he was witness again, this time to the sound of the heavy tread of a man walking about the room in leather boots, although there was nothing to be seen.

Epworth Rectory in Lincolnshire was the birthplace of Methodist leader John Wesley – perhaps one of Britain's most famous clergymen and a man whose teachings now form the

BELOW: *Epworth Rectory, in Lincolnshire, scene of a celebrated poltergeist disturbance.*

basis of the modern-day United Methodist Church. Built in 1709, the rectory was gifted to John's father Reverend Samuel Wesley by Queen Mary after he dedicated a poem on the life of Christ to her. He was unpopular locally and in 1709, villagers – who disapproved of the Reverend's Hanoverian principles – took action against the Wesleys by setting fire to the building and injuring livestock. However, the building was rebuilt and the Wesleys settled there. Mrs Wesley went on to bear 19 children, 14 of whom died in infancy.

The two months of intense poltergeist infestation which began in December 1716, and which made the building famous, began without any

ABOVE: *Not your typical 'haunted house', but the Rectory at Epworth has had its fair share of ghostly goings on.*

warning and with no apparent trigger. They centred on a disturbed spirit which was nicknamed 'Old Jeffrey' by the family. Sounds echoed through the house each night at around 9.45pm; beginning with subtle sounds like that of a saw on wood, or the turning of a windmill, after 15 minutes they would become stronger, louder and more intense, as if the poltergeist was collecting energies which it would expel throughout the dark hours. The ghost created all manner of havoc including shaking the very foundations of the house itself. Crashing glass, moving furniture and the levitation of a bed, which at the time was occupied by Rev. Wesley's daughter Nancy, was accompanied by the startling sound of clanking chains, knocking and loud bangs. The children of the house, who were extremely scared by the phenomena, speculated that it was caused by local witchcraft, which had been reported in the vicinity. However, modern psychic speculation points toward Mrs Wesley, who was unhappy in her marriage, and daughter Hetty, who hated the rectory and harboured negative feelings toward it. Could the psychological state of either woman have triggered the release of psychokinetic energy in the house?

Trying to communicate with the entity proved futile and while it would mimic knocks and tappings, it always failed to answer questions posed to it. One night, Rev. Wesley, who had hitherto never experienced any of the phenomena reported by his family and servants, first heard the strange knockings coming from the nursery. Following them, he is recorded as shouting out 'Thou deaf and dumb devil, why dost thou frighten these children that cannot answer for themselves? Come to me to my study that am a man!' Old Jeffrey replied in earnest knocking loudly before becoming silent for the rest of the night. But the reverend's challenge was met the following evening when, as he opened the door to his study, it was flung back shut with such force that it almost knocked Samuel to the floor.

After almost eight weeks of torment, the disturbances stopped as suddenly as they had begun, at the end of January 1717. Speculation as to why the haunting occurred and who the poltergeist might have been continue to this day. Was this an externalization of pent-up emotion, which took form within the house, or was it the angry spirit of one who was passing through? The case of the Epworth Poltergeist was never satisfactorily closed and I wonder if there are still strange goings-on from time to time at the rectory? Until recently it was operating as a bed-and-breakfast, offering a good night's rest – I wonder…

THE AMHERST POLTERGEIST
1878

It was on Princess Street in the small town of Amherst, Nova Scotia, that in 1878 a terrifying poltergeist manifestation made its presence felt in the home of the family of Esther Cox, marking the beginning of an ordeal which would become known as the most important case of poltergeist attack in Canadian history. After Esther's death in 1912, author Walter Hubbell published a full account of the incident under the title *The Great Amherst Mystery*, which included a testimonial signed by 16 witnesses that what was written reflected the truth.

Esther lived in a small town house with her brother William, sisters Jennie and Olive, Olive's husband Daniel Teed and their two young children. Also under the same roof was Daniel's brother John and a boarder named Walter Hubbell – an actor who later published the aforementioned book. Conditions for the eight-strong family were cramped, to say the least, with Esther sharing a bed with her sister Jennie. It was in this bed that the first sign that something strange had entered their lives manifested.

One night, screams rang through the house as Jennie and Esther awoke terrified to find a writhing form beneath the bedclothes. At first they assumed it to be a mouse but when no rodent could be discovered the incident was dismissed as being the result of tiredness and over-active imaginations; yet both women had witnessed the same physical thing in their bed, moving around in the dark…

The next night screams pierced the silence once more, although this time the cause wasn't in the bed but underneath it. An old wooden fabric box had begun jumping about, banging itself against the bed. Esther wrenched it from its hiding place and dragged it into the middle of the room. This seemed to 'set it free' and it continued its peculiar behaviour in earnest, jumping about like a demon possessed, each movement eliciting screams from Esther and Jennie and summoning the rest of the household into the room to witness the phenomenon.

These initial incidents, although odd, did not seem to be threatening, as is often the case with poltergeist infestations, but on the third night the behaviour of this unseen entity turned decidedly darker. Esther had felt feverish all day and retired to bed at around 10pm. The Teeds assumed she was sleeping off the illness, but ran to her aid when she began screaming at the top of her voice. Opening the door they were met with a horrific scene. On the bed Esther had turned scarlet and was crying at the top of her voice 'My god! What is happening to me? I'm dying'. Her entire body swelled with a fierce redness. When they touched her, they could feel that her temperature had soared to a hellish blaze and her eyes, almost bulging out of their sockets, exuded a sense of panic mixed with fear and excruciating pain. All at once something seemed to grip her throat and she began coughing and spluttering, unable to get her breath and then, to the sound of four deafening bangs from beneath the bed, she slumped back onto the mattress and fell immediately into a trance-like sleep. The Teed family finally made their way back to their beds, both fearful and confused; but the rest of the night passed without incident.

Early next morning an atmosphere of unease oozed around the house; what would today bring? As the day progressed and twilight began to fall, expectancy built once more, but the night passed without disturbance and Esther slept sweetly in her bed with Jennie. The same occurred the next night, and the following. But then, as they had feared, the terror returned four nights later. As the unseen demon toyed with her flesh, Esther writhed in pain unable to breathe and crying out in pain. The family realized that their sister's problem would not go away, and they called a doctor.

OPPOSITE: Poltergeist disturbances often include the movement of objects such as knives and toys, as shown opposite.

RIGHT: *Poltergeist activity can involve furniture being upended and small items thrown around or laid out.*

The first scientific mind to become involved with the events at Amherst was Dr Carritte. He could find no physical reason for the symptoms described by the terrified Teeds, but agreed to sit with Esther during the night to see what might occur. Little did he know that he would bear witness to the most frightening phenomena so far.

It started with a twitch that caught his eye. Esther was in deep sleep and yet, as he watched in the candlelight, the pillow resting beneath her head was moving, as if it was being pulled one way and then another by unseen hands. Then the sounds began, faint at first but then incredibly loud – bang! Bang! BANG! – echoed through the room as the bedclothes were ripped from Esther's sleeping body and flung across the room. Amazed by what he was seeing, Dr Carritte made notes in his book but was disturbed by a new sound, a scraping as that of a pitchfork on plaster. Rearing his head to the source he watched, aghast, as letters were gouged out of the wall, leaving the clear message 'ESTHER COX! YOU ARE MINE TO KILL'.

The entity had made its intentions clear, and the reality of what was happening was firmly planted in the doctor's mind. He agreed to return the next day to try and help Esther, and investigate further. Activity continued through the daylight hours with vegetables flying through the air inside the house and noises from the roof. Dr Carritte later wrote: 'Honestly sceptical persons were on all occasions soon convinced that there was no fraud or deception in the case. Were I to publish it in a medical journal, as you suggest, I doubt if it would be believed by physicians generally. I am certain I could not have believed such apparent miracles had I not witnessed them'.

Unable to find a cause or solution, despite the doctor's best efforts, Esther turned to spiritualists for an answer and began performing automatic writing in order that she might be able to communicate with her tormentor. Although a crude medium, the writings did appear to work and various messages from a variety of 'spirits' claiming to be responsible for the happenings were forthcoming. The controlling entity called itself Maggie Fisher and described how she had died in 1867 and had been at school with Esther. Maggie was joined at various times by the spirits of Bob and John Nickle, Maggie's sister Mary Fisher, Eliza MacNeal and Peter Teed. Contemporary research conducted by paranormal investigators examining the

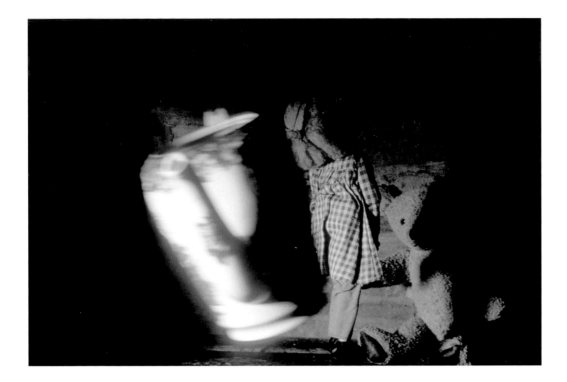

LEFT: *The activity of a poltergeist may also be expressed in the throwing (by invisible agency) of household objects, such as cups, plates, knives, and so on.*

case has suggested that the names, professions and identities of these so-called ghosts should be dismissed as being too similar to people known to Esther.

Whoever or whatever the entity was, its force was now causing other phenomena, apparently with the intention of bringing about Esther's death by one means or another. Knives were thrown with force around the home while lighted matches would manifest out of thin air and drop onto beds. Furniture would levitate and move around, while loud slaps would echo in the night as red finger-marks appeared on Esther's face. As the phenomena grew more intense, Esther's desperation mounted. After sewing-pins had appeared and proceeded to fly into her face, and a pocket-knife was whipped out of the hand of a neighbour and stabbed into her back, Esther turned to the church for help. But even the power of the Baptist faith was no match for the evil poltergeist. As Esther sat in her pew, knockings and banging erupted around the church, drowning out the minister and causing Esther to leave, knowing herself to be the cause.

News of the terrors had now spread, and the landlord of the Teed household became worried about the potential damage to his property that the presence of these tenants might cause. He served an eviction notice, ordering them to leave his property. Esther moved out, hoping that her family would be left in peace. They were, but the entity had other plans for her; it first followed her to a neighbour's house, wreaking havoc on their household, before she finally moved far away to a farm in Brockton, Massachusetts. This attempt at a new life was also thwarted by the power of the unseen being that was attached to Esther, and after a barn burned to the ground, she was blamed and convicted of arson. Esther Cox received a four-month jail sentence, but served only one month before being freed.

After constant terror for months on end, the jail sentence seemed to have a dispelling effect on the entity. After Esther's release the happenings all but ceased, with just a minor incident very occasionally. At last Esther was free from the unwanted intrusion into her life by her unseen tormentors. After marrying twice, Esther Cox died in 1912, aged 53. The mystery of what happened in Amherst, and why it targeted an innocent young woman, has never been explained. The case has baffled the experts who have tried to investigate it, and continues to be an enduring – and troubling – tale of the unexplained.

THE MOST HAUNTED HOUSE IN ENGLAND

28 July 1900 – February 1939

ABOVE: *Borley Rectory, as seen from the air.*

BELOW: *The church at the tiny hamlet of Borley is said to be the current haunt of the village's ghostly residents.*

This haunting came to the public's attention with a sensationalist article in the *Daily Mirror* national newspaper declaring 'ghosts at a haunted rectory'. Seventy-eight years on, the truth is still unknown. Borley Rectory, a rambling remote house in the tiny hamlet of Borley, near Sudbury in Suffolk, was pushed into the paranormal limelight by investigative journalist and ghost hunter Harry Price. It was to become dubbed 'Britain's Most Haunted House' after a book of the same name was published by Price, chronicling the startling events that occurred there.

The rectory was built by Reverend Henry Dawson Bull in 1862 as a family home for himself, his wife and their children. He was the local vicar for the parish, with his church situated across the road next to the grounds of the house. It was during his incumbency that the first known sighting of Borley's most infamous spirit was made. It happened on 28 July 1900, and was watched by Henry's four excited daughters. They described how a shimmering figure had floated down the path in the grounds which subsequently became known as the 'Nun's Walk', as the figure's clothing was described as resembling a nun's habit. The first suggestion that the house was haunted was made in 1885, but the appearance of the nun was heralded as the first proof of ghosts at Borley.

It was the reverend himself who was to see the next phantom, that of a coach and horses driven by a headless coachman, which swept past the house on misty nights. It didn't take long for a legend combining the two visual apparitions to develop. The tale went that, in

medieval times, a nun from a local convent from nearby Bures had tried to elope with a monk from a monastery which had stood on the grounds where the rectory was now located. The pair had been aided by an accomplice who planned to whisk them off to a new life together in a coach and horses from Borley. They were caught, and as punishment the nun, later named as 'Marie Lairre', was entombed alive in a wall at the monastery. The monk was hanged.

The legend has persisted and is probably one of the most well-known ghost stories in the United Kingdom. However, whether any of it can be proven is not clear. There is no evidence of a monastery ever having stood on the rectory site, but there is evidence to suggest a manor house may have been in existence there as early as 1065. Centuries later, Borley Manor was inhabited by Sir Edward Waldegrave, who was executed for heresy in 1561. It is unlikely, according to scholars of religion, that a nun would have been walled up alive in medieval England for this kind of crime, though this is known to have happened in some other countries. It has been suggested by many that there is no truth whatsoever in the tale of the nun and the monk – however, the ghostly nun has been glimpsed many times, including recently.

When Reverend Henry Bull died, his son Harry succeeded him in the living at

ABOVE: *The gate leading to Borley Rectory, once the most haunted house in England.*

Borley, and the Bulls continued their 70-year-long tenancy of the sprawling house. Following the Bulls' time at Borley, the rectory was left unoccupied for a number of years and it was at this stage in its history that stories of ghosts really came to the fore. Villagers avoided the house at night and some said they saw phantoms peering from the windows and a light in an upstairs room. The reputation of this gloomy building as a 'haunted house' was now well established.

In 1928 the Reverend G.E. Smith accepted the living and moved into the house with his family. It had been difficult to find someone to replace Henry Bull and according to records 12 clergymen had turned down the opportunity to serve in the village. It has been speculated that this might have been due to the paranormal reputation the house had by now acquired, but perhaps it was more likely down to the fact that there was no electricity supply and the plumbing was inadequate. In either case, Reverend Smith was not prone to belief in the supernatural – the only ghost he believed in was the Holy one – and was thus unafraid of his new home – at least at the outset.

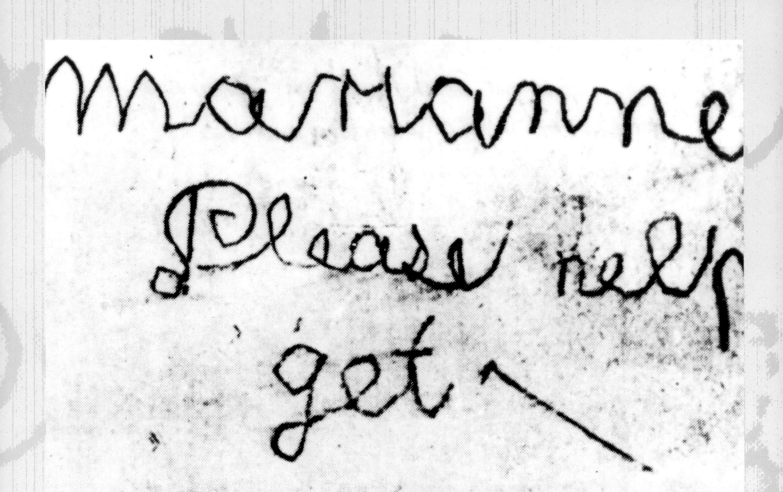

ABOVE: *Messages from the spirits appealed for 'help' in this now famous story.*

Harry Price was called in by the *Daily Mirror* to investigate – and write a piece on – several reports of ghostly encounters that had been made by the Smiths over a number of months, including mysterious footsteps, the sound of a woman shouting 'Don't Carlos, Don't', and a variety of poltergeist-like behaviours, which included smashing crockery and the banging of doors by unseen hands. In addition to the usual phenomena, a strange crude writing appeared on walls throughout the rectory, and bells could be heard ringing even though no such bells existed.

Price first visited the rectory on 12 June 1929, with his secretary Lucie Kaye. As he examined the large rooms of the building, the sound of bells ringing was heard, and later a candlestick was hurled at the ghost hunter from the staircase. Despite not having a medium present, Harry decided to hold an impromptu séance in the Blue Room – a hotbed of this strange activity. As Price and Lucie joined hands with the Smiths, the faint sound of tapping was heard from various areas of the room. Later this became a method of communication with the alleged 'spirit', which identified itself as the ghost of Reverend Harry Bull, who had died in the house.

The Smiths left Borley Rectory on 15 July 1929. The increasing ghostly activity coupled with the uncomfortable nature of the house as a home forced them out, but Harry Price continued his investigations, visiting as frequently as he could and beginning to build up a dossier of the activity he had witnessed.

The next rector didn't arrive until October 1930, over a year after the Smiths left. He was Reverend Lionel Algernon Foyster and he was accompanied by his young wife Marianne and their children. They were soon troubled by the ghosts and invited Price to return to resume his investigation. Much of the activity centred on Marianne, and critics have suggested that she made up many of her claims, being bored in the countryside, married to a man many years older than her, and with few friends to keep her company. When Price arrived he found that the paranormal activities, which Lionel had recorded in a diary, were much more violent and frequent than during the Smiths' time in the house. Messages, apparently from the spirits, were scrawled across walls appealing for 'Light Mass' and 'Please Help'. Between 1930 and 1935, when the Foysters finally left, Lionel recorded more than 2,000 incidents of ghostly activity in his diary.

Price seized the chance to immerse himself in the Borley hauntings after the rector left, arranging to lease the building for 12 months in 1937. He then placed an advert in the national press for people of an inquiring mind to contact him to take part in a long-term ghost hunt at the house. He received more than 200 replies and accepted 40 of them as his ghost hunters. They stayed at the house on a rota system, and were equipped and briefed by Price. He gave them a small blue book in which Price had written a set of instructions on how to conduct the investigation. The investigators were told to note everything that occurred, but despite initial enthusiasm many dropped out very quickly, having witnessed no apparitions at Borley.

Many of his assistants claimed psychic abilities, notably Sidney Glanville and his son Roger and daughter Helen. Through numerous séances held in the house, they contacted a variety of different spirits who each told their story. 'Father Enoch' was a medieval monk who had been buried in the grounds of the rectory, while 'Marie Lairre' was a young novice nun who had been tempted from Le Havre in France to England by an influential member of the Waldegrave family and had been strangled at Borley in 1667. Her remains, she said, were hidden beneath the cellar of the rectory and she wanted them moved to consecrated ground. The claims made by the Glanvilles have been closely scrutinized and have not stood up to scientific analysis. However, some of the communications are interesting to say the least. An entity naming itself 'Sunex Amures' threatened to burn down the rectory at 9pm on 27 March 1938. The night passed with no sign of damage, but strangely the rectory did burn down almost a year later in February 1939.

BELOW: *An early picture of the Borley Rectory. The window on the left on the second floor of the building belongs to the allegedly haunted Blue Room.*

It was a cold February night when Captain William H. Gregson, the tenant of Borley Rectory – which he had renamed Borley Priory – was sorting through some books in the hallway. In a freak accident that was to spell the end of the building forever, a book fell from a pile and struck a paraffin lamp, igniting the room in flame and sending its occupant running for his life. The Blue Room – noted as the 'most haunted' – was the first to burn, and as the villagers watched the infamous house slowly crumble amid the blaze, faces of the spirits were glimpsed watching from the windows. The nearest fire service was miles from this remote corner of the Essex countryside, and when help finally arrived, it was too late to save the rectory – the most haunted house in Britain was no more.

An important piece of this paranormal jigsaw was yet to be discovered by Price when, while sifting through the ruins of the cellar, fragments of a human jawbone and skull were found three feet down; they were later identified as those of a young woman. Was this the proof that Marie Lairre existed, as had been communicated through a séance held by the Glanvilles years earlier? Price arranged for the remains to be interred at Liston churchyard by Reverend Alfred Henning on the evening of 29 May 1945, where they still rest today.

Throughout its 77-year existence, the sinister rectory at Borley was a fascination for the nation, a tourist attraction, a family home and the centre of the haunted world in Britain. Following its destruction, the stories of ghosts have not been laid to rest, with reports of apparitions first in the ruins, and subsequently on the land, where today several bungalows stand. The Nun's Walk is now incorporated into several private gardens and there are no remains of the famous Rectory to be seen. Some paranormal experts have argued that the ghostly activity has now moved across the road to the church, where the nun has been seen, and other phenomena have been witnessed, including ghostly organ music emanating from

BELOW: *The Dining Room at Borley Rectory boasted an intricately carved fireplace with friezes of two monks on either side of the hearth.*

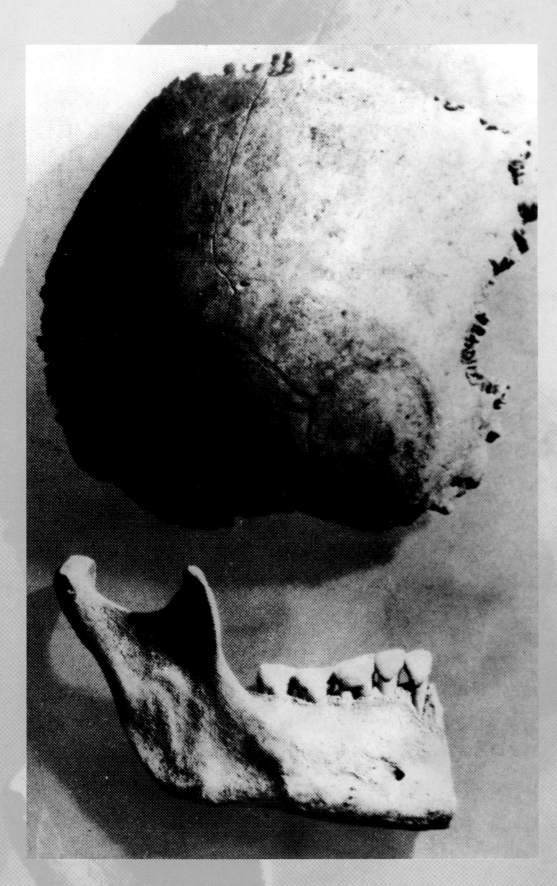

LEFT: *Human bone fragments, thought to be those of 'Marie Lairre', were found in the cellar of the Rectory after it burned down in 1939.*

the locked and empty building. So was Borley Rectory simply an elaborate exaggeration by an unscrupulous showman, as some have described Price, or was it a genuinely haunted house, the like of which has never been seen again? The answer is disputed to this day.

THE REAL STORY BEHIND THE EXORCIST
January–April 1949

The world-renowned sensational horror film *The Exorcist*, written for the screen by William Peter Blatty, was released in 1973 to rave reviews. Following the success of his earlier best-selling novel in 1971, Blatty hit a sure-fire winner when his blend of classic poltergeist phenomena, religious fanaticism and satanic disfiguration hit the screen. Now recognized as one of the greatest films of all time, and recently re-released in 2000, *The Exorcist* has always been at the centre of paranormal controversy. From the start it was hailed as 'based on true events', but the actual events upon which the novel, and later the film were based, were quite different to what most sources reveal. The book and subsequent film revolve around the demonic possession of a young girl, whereas the real account centres on a 13-year-old boy, now known in the annals of psychic research as 'Rob Doe'. For years various authors and journalists have misreported the facts, but an extensive research project carried out by journalist Mark Opsasnick in the late 1990s means that the truth behind one of the world's most famous cases can now be shared.

Born in 1935, Rob Doe grew up in Cottage City, Washington DC. Anecdotes reported in *Strange Magazine* collected from friends and neighbours indicate that he was a loner and had

RIGHT: *Roman Catholic exorcism has a lengthy heritage, as can be seen in this crude old carving of a priest 'casting out' a demon.*

a problematic upbringing in a dysfunctional family. It was in January 1949 that the supernatural world touched Rob and his family for the first time, beginning with inexplicable scratching noises emanating from the ceilings of their home. After the possibility of rats was ruled out, the sounds evolved into footsteps. Objects in the house also started moving, and thoughts of a paranormal presence crept into the family's consciousness – but their journey to the other side had just begun.

The incidents escalated until Rob was attacked for the first time in his bedroom. His bed shook violently – with no apparent cause – and the

bedclothes were ripped from his body. In a desperate attempt to cleanse the house, Rob's mother appealed to the local Lutheran minister, Luther Schulze, for help. Prayers were said in the home and in the local church to rid the house and the boy of the tormenting spirit, but the attempts were to no avail. The noises and disturbances continued unabated – so much so that Rob was unable to rest at night, lying awake in his bed awaiting the arrival of the demon.

In February 1949, Luther requested permission for Rob to spend a night at his house in an attempt to give him some respite from the spirit, but this was fruitless as the presence followed him to the new abode, rattling his bed and tipping him from an armchair, which moved about the room in Luther's presence.

A new line of thought suggested that Rob's mental and psychological condition might be affecting his physical world and to this end it was recommended that he be examined by a mental health clinic. Initially this created a severe reaction from Rob, whose behaviour became even wilder, but when lesions began appearing on his skin – made apparently not by himself but by some exterior entity – he was sent to St Louis Hospital for observation by experts. Under surveillance, the apparent possession continued, gaining momentum with the addition of copious amounts of phlegm exuding from his mouth and a constant stream of drool.

It wasn't until April that Rob's behaviour began to improve. He was introduced to a Jesuit priest who diagnosed 'possession by demons', and an exorcism was granted. It is possible that the Jesuits combined forces with Luther Schulze and an Episcopal priest who took turns performing the rite, which after several weeks was deemed a success.

There have been many publications, articles, television specials and websites about this story, each declaring theirs is the 'true' version of events. In all honesty, no-one can be quite sure; the locations of the diaries kept by the exorcists at the time are unknown. In summary, the real story, while not being as dramatic as the Hollywood version, contains some disturbing facts which cannot easily be explained, and gives food for thought about the real possibility of possession by outside forces.

ABOVE: *The film* The Exorcist *became a box office hit, but the true story is very different from its screen adaptation.*

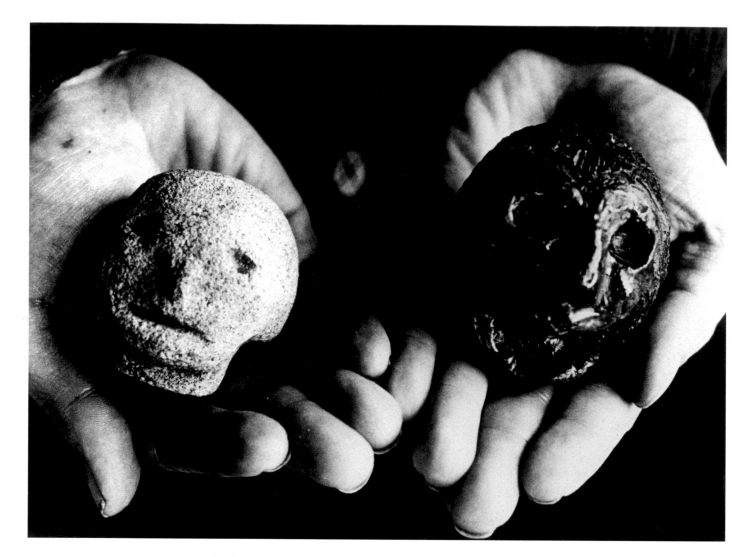

THE HEXHAM HEADS
February 1972

The strange case of the Hexham Heads began in February 1972, when two young children playing in their garden in Hexham, Northumberland, stumbled across two apparently ancient relics amongst the undergrowth. Upon examination, they appeared to be two carved stone heads, each a little smaller then tennis balls. One had a distinctly skull-like male appearance, and the other, slightly smaller head, displayed a more feminine face; both had uneasy expressions that exuded a peculiar melancholy. The heads were crudely finished with hollow eyes and protruding noses and were taken at once into the family home where they were proudly displayed as curiosities.

It was soon after they had been welcomed into the house that they began to take on a life of their own. The family first witnessed that they moved of their own accord, turning from where they had been placed to 'watch' a different area of the house. Household items were found inexplicably broken and a bed was discovered strewn with broken glass from an unknown origin.

The apparent power exuding from the eerie relics was not confined to the house in which they were 'visiting', as the next door neighbours found out a few days later. It was late at night when the mother of the house was awoken from her sleep by her young daughter, who was in terrible pain from a toothache and needed comforting from her mother. It was while they were talking that the power of the heads momentarily came into their lives with an incredible encounter with what they described as a werewolf…

Both mother and daughter heard a sound on the landing and as they strained their eyes in the gloom they both watched as a half-man, half-beast crossed the threshold. Frightened for their lives they screamed out in terror, at which point the father came running into the room, but he was too late to witness the manifestation as it had already bounded down the staircase to the floor below. All three stood in silence as the man-beast could be heard padding around, before the house became silent and normality returned. The front door had been unlocked and they assumed that this extraordinary creature had left by that means, never to return again.

Following this remarkable encounter with what appeared to be a crypto-zoological marvel, the heads were given to a Southampton-based historian of Celtic culture. No doubt the family was glad to be rid of them, hoping their lives, which had been temporarily touched by the supernatural world, would return to normal. According to the accounts of this bizarre tale, the historian declared that the heads were indeed of Celtic origin and resembled similar finds that she had collected from other sources; she dated them at over 1,800 years old. She had been given no details pertaining to the weird phenomena that seemed to be caused by the presence of the heads, which is why her own report is of great interest.

Several nights after taking possession of the heads and adding them to her existing collection, she was disturbed in the night by the presence of what she described as a half-man, half-animal standing in the doorway of her bedroom. She said 'it was about six feet high, slightly stooping and it was black against the white door. It was half-man, half-animal; the upper part being that of a wolf and the lower of a man. It was covered in a very dark fur'. As the creature disappeared out of the bedroom the historian leapt from her bed – compelled to follow it, she earnestly pursued the creature as it descended the staircase and departed from the house. Following this first encounter the werewolf appeared several more times and was seen by other members of her family, often on the staircase where on one occasion it jumped over the banister and landed in the hall. Other phenomena which had not begun until the heads had entered the building included the anomalous slamming of doors and the sound of the beast padding about – although no visual manifestation accompanied the sound. It was thought that the Hexham Heads were responsible for causing the plethora of sinister encounters and it was decided that they should be removed from the building, along with the historian's entire collection.

Soon afterwards the Hexham Heads passed into the hands of another collector whose identity and current whereabouts are unknown. Did the power of the heads only have a limited lifespan? Or is the beastly guardian still guarding these ugly carvings? Have we seen the last of this gruesome twosome? Or will they rear their ugly heads once more…?

BELOW: *A terrifying manifestation of a 'wolf-like' being was triggered by the Hexham Heads in Southampton.*

HIGH HOPES – THE WORLD'S MOST INFAMOUS HAUNTED HOUSE

November 1974 – May 2006

On the evening of 13 November 1974, the New York police were called to 112 Ocean Avenue, Amityville on Long Island, where six people had been killed in a brutal mass murder. This tragedy was the beginning of one of the most infamous, controversial and enduring supernatural stories the world has ever seen. In 1975, the Lutz family moved into the house and claim they endured 28 days of terror at the hands of apparitions and demons, finally fleeing in the middle of the night, leaving all their worldly possessions and vowing never to return. Their story was the basis of a book by Jay Anson titled *The Amityville Horror*, which became an international bestseller. It spawned a film of the same name in 1979, which was followed by eight further films, the latest being the remake of the original in 2005. The name 'Amityville' is now synonymous with horror and fear throughout the world, but how did this Dutch Colonial suburban house find itself at the centre of the haunted world?

Upon arrival at 112 Ocean Avenue, the investigating officers encountered a horrific scene – the bloodstained bodies of six members of the Italian De Feo family. Ronald De Feo Senior, his wife Louise, their daughters Dawn and Alison and their sons Mark and nine-year-old John Matthew lay dead, face-down in their beds; each had been shot at close range by a 3.5-calibre Marlin rifle. With no apparent motive for the killing – the family was respected in the community and lead a 'normal' life – suspicions turned on the remaining member of the family, 23-year-old Ronny, who was known to have a mean streak and was a self-confessed drug user. At first, blame was shifted onto the mafia, with whom Mr De Feo had previous connections when living in the Brooklyn area, but later under questioning, Ronny confessed, describing how he had crept from room to room, shooting each and every member of his family in cold blood. When searching for a motive, police were confused when Ronny explained that 'the voices' had told him to do it. Suspecting insanity, they called in psychiatrist Harold Zolan to examine De Feo. He found that while Ronny suffered from a personality disorder and problems with drug abuse, he was fully aware of his actions at the time and subsequently De Feo was convicted of the murders and is currently serving six 25-year sentences for his crimes. According to reports, he has always maintained that he was 'compelled' to commit the murders by demonic forces, which he believed to be present inside the house on Ocean Avenue.

Upon examination of the case, which is continually misreported in various media, it is clear that there were underlying issues within the De Feo family before the events of 13 November. According to some sources, Mr De Feo had sought the help of a Catholic priest weeks before the killings in an attempt to calm the troubled household which he had named 'High Hopes' when he moved in. He had surrounded the building with religious icons and statuary, allegedly telling enquirers he had done so 'because I have the Devil on my back'. Speculation as to whether he was referring to his son Ronny – who was experiencing severe problems with drug use and whose behaviour was escalating out of control – or to the Devil incarnate is unclear. De Feo's wife Louise seems to have exhibited some degree of a sixth-sense, telling a housekeeper that a tragedy would befall her family well before it actually did.

In the ensuing 30 years of this enduring case, many different avenues of investigation have been undertaken, and numerous suggestions and conclusions have been made, many focussing on the land beneath the house itself, which is believed to be cursed. Interestingly, before the present house was built on the site in 1924, a house dating from 1782 stood on

OPPOSITE: *A still from the film* The Amityville Horror, *showing the film's depiction of the Nightmare House.*

ABOVE: *George and Kathy Lutz (as depicted in the original film) recorded a terrifying diary of events while residing in this house of horrors.*

the land, but it was dismantled and moved to another part of Amityville, because – according to eminent parapsychologist Hans Holzer – continuous problems of a supernatural nature were experienced. Even further back in time legend has it that the original Indian settlers, the Montaukett tribe, chose this site because of a latent 'power' and used the land to bury their enemies face-down – so that they would stare forever into Hell itself. This obviously resonates with the fact that the De Feo family members were found dead, face-down in their beds.

The story becomes more complicated with the arrival of John Ketcham, supposedly a settler who fled Salem at the time of the witch trials in 1692 and came to Amityville – possibly to Ocean Avenue. Some say he continued his witchery and that he is buried on the site. Historical records do indicate that such a man existed, but whether he was connected with Salem and practised the dark arts is pure conjecture and has added yet another layer of mystery to this already complex case.

It is important to note that the Amityville Historical Society refute any claims of the former house being moved because of ghostly disturbances, and most residents of the coastal village do not believe in the alleged 'horror' of Ocean Avenue. It is understandable that locals would want to dismiss the 'brand' that is 'Amityville', as hoards of drunken teenagers, goths, ghost hunters and tourists create a steady stream of unwanted traffic through the locale, particularly around Hallowe'en when, like Salem in Massachusetts and Borley and Pendle Hill in England, the area is inundated with troublemakers.

At the conclusion of the De Feo affair, Amityville residents were ready to put the gruesome memories behind them, but the supernatural legacy of Ocean Avenue had really only just begun. The first question which sparked the interest of psychical researchers was the fact that the gunshots had not been heard by any neighbours. Nor, it seemed, had any members of the De Feo family woken up before they were shot dead. They were all sleeping face down, just like their Montaukett predecessors on the site. So, was a silencer used on the gun, perhaps? Not according to the police investigators assigned to the case. So how was it that the shots went unheard? Hans Holzer suggests that when a strong psychic field is manifest it can affect the way in which sound is perceived, effectively silencing the usual sound from the outside world, as if the house itself was in some kind of psychic cocoon for the duration of Ronny's alleged possession. He also suggests that the influence of the house had, over time, infected Ronny with its intention, requiring 'life' as a kind of food for its continued survival. This may sound like a far-fetched theory, and yet the same thing has been concluded at other buildings around the world. Similar experiences have led investigators to believe that buildings themselves can become structurally possessed with an intelligent malignant force, or *genius loci,* the 'spirit of the place'.

In early September 1975, George and Kathy Lutz, who had recently married, were looking for a new home. George needed somewhere to base his surveying business and Kathy wanted a happy home for her three children from her previous marriage to grow up in. When they were introduced to 112 Ocean Avenue they had no idea that they were about to enter a nightmare that would change their lives forever. After viewing the house and falling in love with it, they were told of its troubled past. This was reflected in the heavily reduced price tag, but did not put off the Lutzes – they went into the eye of the storm with their eyes wide open.

With the house sign 'High Hopes' still swinging in the breeze 13 months after the De Feo murders, the Lutz family moved into their new home. A close friend made Kathy and George promise that they would have the house blessed, and so they called in Catholic priest Father Ralph Pecoraro, or 'Father Ray' as they knew him. At the end of the blessing Father Ray turned to George and told them not to use the sewing room on the first floor as a bedroom. At the time he told them only that he felt uncomfortable in there and that they should not spend too much time in that room. Much later it emerged that Father Ray had been the first to witness incredible physical and audible phenomena – after he had sprinkled Holy Water in the room a loud deep voice had shouted 'Get Out!' from behind him, before slapping him across the face. He was alone in the room at the time.

It was Kathy who first sensed something wrong in the house; it began after the Christmas festivities of 1975 with the sounds of scraping and banging around the building. Coupled with glimpses of 'movements' in their peripheral vision the family began to experience other phenomena which they could not explain. Tension mounted quickly as each member of the family experienced their own version of nightmarish events. George was gripped by an intense icy cold sensation and became obsessed with building the fire in the drawing room, ensuring that a constant blaze kept the house uncomfortably warm.

Missy, Kathy's youngest daughter, had been assigned the bedroom at the top of the house where she developed a relationship with an invisible friend. George and Kathy took little notice of this until one day Missy asked, 'Can angels speak?', to which Kathy replied that they could. Missy then said that she had one in her room, that it was called 'Jody' and looked like a pig with bright red eyes. She went on to say that it could become invisible. Jody had told Missy that, 'she would always live in this house', which made Kathy and George fearful that they were not in control of what was happening around them.

Other phenomena including the front door slamming in the middle of the night – even though it was closed and locked shut – and the sound of a 'marching band' heard downstairs while George was in bed, indicated that the 'presence' was gathering strength. The personalities of the family were gradually changing and it was Kathy who tried to summon Father Ray back to the property to help. Her attempts to communicate with him were inhibited by technical problems on the telephone line, even though calls to other people could be made without a problem. It was later discovered that the priest was loathe to return to the house, as he was experiencing physical 'warnings'. Whenever he discussed with colleagues in a nearby church the possibility of returning to the house, he felt cold spots around him.

In the grip of winter, the phenomena continued in earnest, the power of the 'presence' now rooted firmly within the combined psyche of the terrified family. It was in early 1976 that Kathy made a frightening discovery in the basement. An old shelving

BELOW: *The now legendary 'eye windows' of 'High Hopes' have now been removed from the house on Ocean Avenue, thereby discouraging annoying tourists from visiting the property.*

ABOVE: *The 2005 version of the film* The Amityville Horror *was the most graphic yet, and was less factual than fictional.*

unit had been left *in situ* by the De Feos and Kathy decided that she wanted to use it in another part of the house. Shifting it towards the staircase she noticed a small doorway had been uncovered and calling George, the pair reached into the gloom to discover a tiny room daubed with what appeared to be red paint. A disgusting pungent odour emitted from the empty space and the Lutzes' dog cowered as if being challenged by an unseen intruder when brought down into the basement to investigate. After examining early plans of the house, the Lutzes discovered that the room was not marked – so why was it built, and for what purpose? Was this, as has been suggested, the corrupt heart of a troubled house? Did some terrible deed in the past pave the way for what was happening in George and Kathy's present? And did this same force influence the actions of Ronny De Feo, as he still claims to this day?

Sceptics have asked why the Lutzes did not leave sooner if they were experiencing such frightening phenomena as they claim. George responded that they were unable to leave – all their combined finances had been tied up in the purchase of the house and there was no alternative available – and so they stayed put. Other experiences on record include the manifestation of thousands of flies in the sewing room even though this was the middle of winter, the sighting by George of 'Jody' looking out of Missy's bedroom, the discovery of cloven hoof marks in fresh snow outside the windows of the house, and the temporary physical transformation of Kathy into an old hag. George began waking every night at 3.15am – later found to be the time of the De Feo killings – and Kathy was plagued by dreams in which she re-experienced the murders, made disturbingly real when her accounts of what happened that night matched exactly with previously unreleased police records. Friends also witnessed various supernatural phenomena when visiting the Lutzes. Testimonies from these other individuals added credence to the Lutzes' version of events and stymied those who tried to dismiss their story.

By now the opinions of psychic researchers and mediums were being sought by the family. Ed and Lorraine Warren were enlisted as investigators on the case and together with other researchers they began an intensive study of the house. Much of this pointed back to the legend of the Indian settlers. It was suggested that George and Kathy perform their own exorcism of the property and to this end they walked from room to room reciting the Lord's Prayer in the hope of dispelling the negative forces. This action only provoked the phenomena, seemingly angering the house and ensuring that it turned up the heat on the Lutz family in a defiant show of its merciless power.

In George's words the building had become 'uninhabitable' and so, after one last night of fear George, Kathy and their three children fled the house for Kathy's mother's home, leaving their possessions behind – and taking only a cedar box made by George's grandfather. The experiences of that final night in 112 Ocean Avenue remained a closely guarded secret kept by George and Kathy up until their deaths, their testimony being too frightening to relive. What is known is that the walls of the house itself seemed to come alive as they ran down the staircase to escape. George took one last glimpse up to the landing before he slammed the front door shut behind him – to see a tall hooded figure in white which raised its finger to point at him.

After leaving Amityville, the Lutzes maintained that some remnant of the evil force followed them to Kathy's mother's house, where it caused the levitation and another temporary transfiguration of Kathy into an old woman. It also followed them to California where they began a new life, troubling them only from time to time. Once settled, they recorded a series of tapes of their experiences in a cathartic process to help them move beyond the events that had ripped their lives into tatters. It was these tapes that were the basis of Jay Anson's book, and subsequently the first film. During the 1980s, the couple divorced but remained on good terms. Kathy claimed in a television interview in 2000 that they had both continued to be disturbed separately after their divorce, until an exorcist, *allegedly* connected to the Archbishop of Canterbury, gave them a remote blessing – which finally left them in peace.

Kathy Lutz died on 17 August 2004 of emphysema, while George passed away on 8 May 2006. To the end of their lives they both continued to respond to sceptics, claiming to the very end that it had not been a hoax. In his last television interview for The History Channel, George said, 'Whatever was there was very intelligent, very impatient. Its abilities are more powerful than we really understand'. Regardless of whether every aspect of the story is the truth, or elements of fiction have become incorporated over 30 years, the legacy of the Amityville haunting remains the most absorbing and terrifying account of the power of the paranormal in the world today.

THE ENFIELD POLTERGEIST
30 August 1977–September 1978

The most famous case of a poltergeist infestation in the UK has to be that which happened in a small suburb of London in 1977, and continued until September 1978. The case is referred to now as 'The Enfield Poltergeist' and centred around a divorcee named Peggy Harper and her four children, Rose, Janet, Pete and Jimmy. What started out as the movement of objects and audible phenomena soon escalated into a high-profile case, which included, at its height, temporal possession and fire phenomena.

The poltergeist arrived one warm night in August, when Peggy was called into the bedroom at the back of their small home, which was shared by 11-year-old Janet and 10-year-old Pete. The children had experienced their beds jolting up and down of their own accord, which they described to their mother as the beds 'going all funny'. However, by the time she had arrived there was nothing to be seen.

It was at 9.30pm the following night that she was summoned once again to the bedroom; this time it was 'shuffling sounds' which had been heard by Janet and Pete. Thinking that it might be the chair moving around, Peggy picked it up and carried it downstairs, hoping that they would settle and return to sleep, but as she made her way out of the room and turned off the light she too heard a strange sound. It was as if someone was lazily walking around the bedroom in a pair of slippers. She immediately switched the light back on and the sound stopped. Puzzled she turned the light out once more, at which point the sounds continued. Next there were four loud knockings which seemed to emanate from within the wall that connected the house to next door. Then an incredible display of poltergeist behaviour was

BELOW: *This teapot was distorted by an unseen force of power thought by some to have been a Poltergeist.*

witnessed by all three, as a heavy chest of drawers moved away from the wall of its own volition. In an act of defiance Peggy walked over to the chest and pushed it back into position, but no sooner had she turned around than it was pushed away from the wall again. This time Peggy was unable to move it – as if some unseen thing was blocking it, or pushing it from the other side. Confused and frightened, Peggy told the children to put on their dressing gowns and go downstairs while she collected the other children from her own bedroom. Within minutes they were all trudging across the street to a neighbour's house, leaving their home, and its new inhabitant, alone.

The first course of action was for the neighbours to see if they could find an explanation for what Peggy had described. As they crossed the threshold they could hear the noises Peggy and the children had heard – loud knocking coming from within the very fabric of the walls themselves. Unable to find any reason for the sound they called the local police station, and police officers were sent to investigate. One of the officers was witness to the phenomena that were occurring; he watched amazed as a chair slid across the floor towards him – even though there was no-one else in the room at the time.

ABOVE: *Psychic investigator Maurice Grosse displays a collection of items manipulated by the Poltergeist in Enfield.*

After realising that the police could offer no help, Peggy turned to a local vicar and subsequently a medium, seeking their help. She also contacted the press to see if they could help her find someone who could rid the house of the haunted happenings. The *Daily Mail* sent a reporter and photographer to investigate, and while taking a picture the photographer received a sharp jab in the head after a Lego brick was thrown at him by an invisible force. The result was a deep bruise that lasted over a week.

The reporter, George Fallows, called in The Society for Psychical Research, who selected Maurice Grosse, a paranormal investigator, to look into the case. Together with colleague Guy Lyon Playfair, he studied it for more than two years as the primary researcher and, with Playfair, collaborated on a book entitled *This House is Haunted*, which tells the story in great detail.

On 8 September, just a few days after he first became involved with the Harper family and their poltergeist, Maurice had his first glimpse of what was to unfold over the coming months. A chair was projected four feet across Janet's bedroom while she lay sleeping; it was unseen the first time, but on the second occasion Grosse and three representatives from the *Daily Mirror* were lying in the room waiting – and caught the chair moving on camera.

As the phenomena escalated and pressure was placed on the house to 'perform' for the media it was discovered that some of the incidences – banging on pipes, for example – were manufactured by Janet. Sceptics are quick to use this to dismiss everything that happened in the case, saying the entire episode was a hoax created by one or more of the children. But this does not explain the moving items, sounds and projectiles, which could not have been easily faked because they occurred in Janet's presence, where others could observe that she was doing nothing to make them happen.

The most compelling part of this story took place later in the case when Janet began to become temporarily possessed after she had entered a deep, trance-like state. A voice, described as that of a very old man, seemed to speak 'through' her and discuss various things with investigator Maurice Grosse. The entity told Grosse that he had died in the house 53 years earlier and was called 'Bill'. The voice of the entity was recorded on many occasions and is a chilling sound to behold whether you are a believer or not. Maurice approached a voice

ABOVE: *A section of pipe was bent by the Poltergeist during the haunting, showing its sheer brute force and great strength.*

coach for a deep analysis of the voice produced by Janet and it was discovered that it had been made not by the usual vocal chords, but by the 'second chords' which, usually, are not used during speech. Actors can be trained to use these chords to produce a very gravelly sound, as Janet had done, yet with great pain and only in short bursts. Janet had spoken in this way for several hours at a time with no apparent effect on her 'normal' voice.

The levitations of Janet, also controversial, have not been fully explained. Several famous photographs show Janet in mid-flight across her bedroom, allegedly being hurled by the entity, yet some say she is simply jumping around and fooling those who want to believe. What is not so easy to explain is the testimony of one passer-by who watched through her bedroom window as she was levitated around the room.

When the BBC visited the house to conduct some recordings their equipment was mysteriously affected, and upon inspection had been internally broken. Other things around the house also became subject to the powers of the poltergeist, including spoons that bent in Janet's presence, and a variety of other items including crockery, a pipe and the lid of a metal teapot.

With the hoard of investigators, mediums, media reporters and sightseers that were going through the house, The Society for Psychical Research decided it would be a good idea to have some fresh eyes look at the case, and subsequently Anita Gregory and John Beloff visited the Harper family to make their own enquiries. What they witnessed, and later reported, was a host of trickery which they say was created by Janet. They were not allowed to be in the room when the 'poltergeist' was performing, and had to stand with their backs to Janet and Rose while the 'voice' of the entity spoke. It was clear to these new investigators that the case had devolved into a minefield of confusion and conflicting opinions. Maurice Grosse, whom I have met and believe to be a genuinely objective researcher, concluded that the phenomena, for the most part, were real. Anita and John, on the other hand, dismissed the case as fakery.

Two years after the poltergeist had entered the lives of the Harper family in Enfield it mysteriously disappeared, leaving Peggy and her children to pick up the pieces and try to rebuild their lives. It remains a puzzling high-profile case which cannot be fully explained. What seems to have started out as a genuine case of poltergeist infestation later became embellished by the children who, under great pressure from constant media attention, succumbed to the temptation to create some of the incidences by trickery.

THE GHOST WRITERS
Autumn 1984 – March 1987

It began with a six-toed footprint on a wall in tiny Meadow Cottage in Dodleston near Manchester one evening in late autumn 1984. The remarkable and important tale of the happenings experienced by Ken Webster and various friends, investigators and experts is now considered by many to be one of the most important modern-day records of the powers of the haunted world.

The full account of two years of correspondence between Ken and individuals from other time zones, notably one 'Tomas Harden' from the 16th century, can be found in Ken's excellent book *The Vertical Plane*. Now out of print but available on the second-hand market, it is essential reading for any serious student of the paranormal and stands on a prominent shelf in my library. The story received much attention in the late 1980s and early 1990s, and was serialised by the BBC – unfairly according to Ken – as part of their *Out of This World* programme.

The initial outbreak of phenomena centred on the kitchen area of the building; furniture was upturned, items flung about and a general mess was created by the unseen force,

BELOW: *Strange, old-fashioned script appeared on the floor of a cottage in Dodleston during a bizarre case of communication across time.*

clearly present in the terraced 18th-century cottage on Kinnerton Road. The occurrences could easily be filed as 'classic poltergeist phenomena' (stacking phenomena, noises and objects being thrown) until the first weird twist that was to make this experience stand out against all others as unique.

Ken, a teacher at the local school, had borrowed an early BBC 'B' computer for the weekend. Home computers were unheard of at the time; local area networks, the World Wide Web and modems did not exist. He and Debbie, his girlfriend, had accidentally left the computer switched on one evening when they went out and when they returned a poem addressed directly to Ken, Debbie and their lodger Nicola, had appeared on the screen. Having no hard drive, they immediately saved it to a floppy disk before the computer was returned to the school, putting the inexplicable appearance of the poem down to 'the poltergeist' and thinking no more about it. However, the presence which was trying to contact them did not give up. When Ken borrowed a different computer at a later date, leaving it switched on in the kitchen while they were absent, another anomalous message appeared. Once again, its manifestation on the computer was unexplained, but this time was in a different idiom – an archaic form of English. This second message had a distinctly threatening undertone and concern began to set in.

In order to catch the hoaxer, who it was assumed was responsible for the messages, Ken borrowed another computer and loaded it with a fresh floppy disk upon which no material was recorded. It was placed in the kitchen – where the poltergeist activity was most

ABOVE: *Several poltergeist disturbances took place in the cottage during the various communications across time.*

OPPOSITE: *A BBC computer was the initial link between a man in the 16th century and one in the 20th!*

prevalent – and left turned on in the hope that this would prove the communications were from a 'natural' source. Another message appeared, to which Ken and Debbie replied by typing a message back to the 'ghost writer'.

Uniquely, this was the beginning of a two-way communication between an invisible force – who gave his name as 'Lukas Wainman' – and Ken and Debbie, through a remote BBC computer in their poltergeist-infested kitchen. The effect of the computer's presence seemed to calm the physical phenomena, which ceased while the communications got underway.

In order to try to understand what was happening, Ken involved a friend, Peter Trinder, an expert in English, to see if he could decipher the wording of the messages which were building up to a considerable case file. What perplexed Peter was the fashion in which the messages were linguistically arranged – they did not make sense and indicated a 'mock-Tudor' style, quite different from a genuine piece of writing constructed in the Tudor period.

The Society for Psychical Research became involved at Ken's invitation. After conducting a study they ruled out the possibility that Ken and Debbie were fraudsters – messages appeared on the computer reacting to questions posed by the researchers which were unseen by Ken and Debbie. After conducting their investigation they were unable to offer any explanation for what was happening. The invisible communicator offered the investigators one opportunity to receive replies to pertinent questions put to him/it, but it was not taken. If the SPR investigator was willing to risk losing his soul, the communicator wrote, he would answer his questions – at which point the researcher backed away from the case. Bewildered by the case, the SPR failed to report on what was happening and Ken was left to seek expert help elsewhere. This new aid came in the form of Gary Rowe – a paranormal investigator from Wales whose name and contact information had been given to Ken by a communicator via the computer! The methods used by Gary to investigate did not, however, meet with Ken and Debbie's approval – each investigator seemed more intent on putting questions to the computer, rather than trying to understand the dynamics by which the messages were manifesting.

By now Lukas was not the only entity apparently communicating through time; he had been joined by the mysterious and enigmatically named '2109'. This being claimed to be from the future and, it seems, was responsible for 'editing' the messages that were passing through the space-time continuum. Three other communicators also made contact. Later, by April 1986, message-writing was taken over by 'Tomas Harden' who, it seemed, had lived in a farmhouse on the site of Meadow Cottage in the 16th century.

By March 1987, over 300 messages had been received from various alleged sources, not only through the computer but also scrawled in chalk over the floor and walls of the cottage, and on pieces of paper left about the place. It seemed that over time the power for communicating grew stronger but then, after a few final messages of goodbye, they ceased completely. One further message came through the computer when, badgered by a guest, Ken switched it on in the hope that she would become bored very quickly viewing a blank screen. However, a communication (the contents of which are unknown) did arrive – and shocked her so much that she fainted on the spot and has refused to discuss its contents ever since.

This controversial case has been re-examined by a variety of contemporary experts since the original happenings, including Laura Wright – lecturer in English at Cavendish College, Cambridge – who analysed some of the messages for signs of fraud, for which she found no evidence. It is clear that television programmes featuring this case have been biased towards uncovering a hoax, rather than looking at the wider picture, and I advise any interested party to read Ken's excellent book before passing judgement on this strange and unique episode in paranormal history.

THE HAUNTED COTTAGE

March 1994 – March 1998

The 250-year-old Lowes Cottage at the end of Hollow Lane in the village of Upper Mayfield, Derbyshire, made headline news in March 1998 when its owners of four years claimed that it was haunted. The unquiet ghosts were those of a young boy who had been strung up and killed by hanging from a rafter, and a milkmaid named Ellen, who had been locked in the cellar and starved to death.

The claim made by Andrew and Josie Smith, who had restored the once derelict cottage, was that the vendors had not made them aware of its spectral inhabitants, whose existence was allegedly well known throughout the village. Susan Melbourne, who had sold the Smiths the cottage after inheriting it with her sister from their late father, disputed the claim, saying that she had grown up in the cottage and never heard of any ghostly tales associated with the house. However, the Smiths had obtained legal advice and sued the Melbournes for non-disclosure.

In a unique case the Smiths were given permission by a county-court judge to pursue a civil claim for the return of the £41,000 which they had paid for the house. The Melbournes counter-sued for £3,000 claiming that Andrew and Josie had not yet paid the remainder of the agreed purchase-price of £44,000. Susan is on record as saying 'Basically, they owe us money and are trying to get out of paying it'.

Acting for the prosecution, solicitor Stephen Savage explained to the nation that the principle was the same as if the vendors had not declared faulty plumbing or central heating, adding that his clients, the Smiths, would not have bought the property if they had been made

BELOW: *The phantom of a young boy reputedly haunts Lowes Cottage, along with a milkmaid named Ellen.*

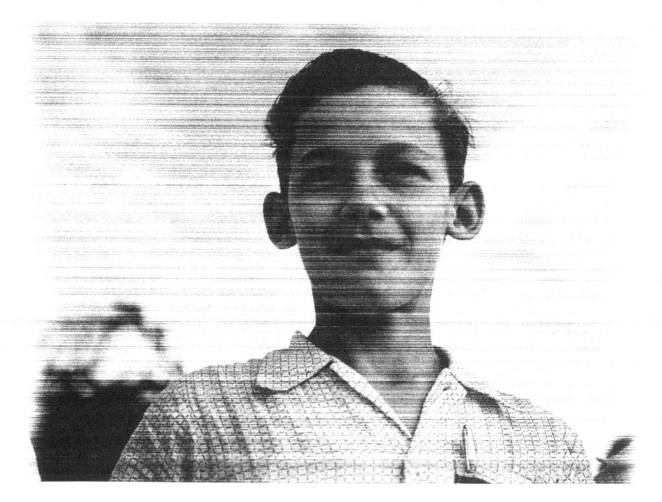

LEFT: *Lowes Cottage, in Upper Mayfield, found itself not only at the centre of a haunting, but also at the centre of a court case!*

ABOVE: *The atmosphere of Lowes Cottage was described as a living hell, and was so thick, according to Andrew Smith, that you could 'lean into it'.*

OPPOSITE: *The house in Hollow Lane has a heritage of haunted happenings, according to one-time owners Andrew and Josie Smith.*

aware of its haunted reputation. At no point in the negotiations did the vendors, or their estate agents, mention ghosts.

After existing in what they described as a 'living hell' invoked by the presence of the spirits, the couple turned to the church for help, enlisting the services of Church of England vicar Reverend Peter Mockford. After visiting the site on several occasions, Rev. Mockford agreed to provide an affidavit in support of their court case, so convinced was he of the presence of supernatural forces within the walls of Lowes Cottage. The Smiths claim that objects were thrown around, and Andrew described the atmosphere as so thick you could 'lean into it'. Josie had also been terrified while lying in bed one night when a pair of unseen hands had seized her by the throat and throttled her, leaving the couple paralysed with fear. Andrew had been unable to work away from home for long as Josie and their three children were too scared to be left alone for any length of time. Rather than conduct the traditional exorcism, which is often carried out by the Catholic Church, Rev. Mockford's approach was to cleanse the house by the use of forceful prayer, but this had only given the Smiths a temporary respite, and following the return of the ghosts they wished to leave for good.

In January 1999, Judge Peter Stretton ruled in favour of the previous owners, Susan Melbourne and her sister Sandra Podmore, saying 'I do not accept that it is haunted now or has been at any other time', and describing the actions of the Smiths as 'extraordinary'. The house has since changed hands and a new owner, who was made fully aware of the 'history' of the house before purchasing it, is now set to contend with the otherworldly inhabitants of Lowes Cottage. So far nothing unusual has been reported – but perhaps we have not heard the last of it?

Chapter 2
Beholding the Spirits

How do the spirits of the dead manifest in our lives through ritual and everyday life? Whether you consider yourself to be a religious person or have no feelings about faith and belief, you will have taken part in celebrations whose basis lies at the very heart of the haunted world.

As you will discover in this chapter, celebrations and holidays the world over are based on ancient philosophies, beliefs and ceremonies, which have been repackaged over the centuries into what we commonly know them as today. Annual festivals such as Christmas and Easter are now generally accepted as Christian holidays, yet in fact they have assimilated these older traditions and borrowed much of their symbolism and imagery. Hallowe'en, or Samhain to give it the correct name, derives not from popular American horror culture as many believe, but from an ancient Celtic end-of-year fire festival. I will also examine other ancient celebrations like Imbolc and Belthane. As you will see, our forefathers, who lived closer to the land, held these annual rites in high regard.

In ancient Rome, the Festival of Lemuria was a time when the dead would walk in our world again, while in China the spooky Festival of the Hungry Ghosts is a chilling reminder that in the past our ancestors sincerely believed that it was necessary to appease the spirits of those who had gone before, lest they wreak their revenge on us. Now lost in time – although sometimes still celebrated by those following older paths of belief – these colourful pageants are remembered here as we behold the spirits…

IMBOLC

FIRE FESTIVAL AND WITCHES' GREATER SABBAT
1 February

The predecessor of the Christianized 'Candlemass', Imbolc is one of the four major Celtic fire festivals in the year, now celebrated as a sabbat in the neo-Pagan 'Wheel of the Year'. Imbolc means literally 'in the belly' and it is associated with fertility because lambs are born at this time of year. In broader terms, this relates to the belief that Mother Nature would bring back the plants, trees and flowers which had been scant through the bitter winter. Also known as *Oimelc* – a Celtic term for 'spring' also meaning 'ewe's milk', for ewes lactate for their newborn at this time of year – the celebration is one of hope. Even though the days are still dark and cold and food is scarce, the nights grow shorter and the determined force of Nature pushes through the icy snow with the first crocus heads.

A folktale from the Isle of Man makes reference to the abundance of milk, naming the festival 'White Brigid's Day'. More than simply a drink, milk was a major source of nourishment for early peoples, and being so precious it was seen as a worthy libation for their gods. Thus it was poured across thresholds or shrines in the hope that it would please the deities and ensure bountiful times ahead. In Ireland the day is known as the Feast of St Brigid.

Celebrations at Imbolc include the lighting of fires, although despite it being a Celtic fire festival, the emphasis is not on the heat the fires produce, but rather on the illumination they provide – celebrating the fact that light has been creeping back each day since Yule and that the change it has brought to the world is now apparent. Mother Nature is renewing herself as the Wheel turns closer towards summer.

Imbolc was very important to the ancient inhabitants of Ireland, as can be seen at the Mound of the Hostages in Tara. Here, an inner chamber is directly aligned with the sunrise at Imbolc and Hallowe'en.

Traditional customs at Imbolc include the lighting of lamps and candles, symbolizing the welcoming of new light into your home and your life. This was later Christianized into 'Candlemass' as celebrated in churches throughout the world. In Irish custom, and now celebrated more widely in neo-Paganism, a corn dolly effigy of Brigid would be made by young girls and placed in a bed specially prepared by their mothers. A wand of ash would be tapped against the doll in this ancient rite of worshipping the female source of Mother Nature, to ensure a fertile life. Hearths would be swept clean on St Brigid's Eve, and in the morning the remnants of ash would be inspected for symbolic markings to see if Brigid had visited the home to bless it for the coming year.

In the modern-day USA, the Groundhog Day custom on 2 February has connections to Imbolc. If a groundhog sees its own shadow on this morning and is shunned back to its burrow in fear, this indicates that there will be six more weeks of winter weather.

PREVIOUS PAGE: *The lusty god, Pan, is worshipped at various festivals of ancient origin throughout the year.*

OPPOSITE: *The lighting of candles is central to the theme of Imbolc – now Christianized as 'Candlemas.'*

BELOW: *The name Imbolc derives from 'Oimelc', an old Celtic word for 'ewe's milk'.*

SETSUBUN
3 February

Meaning 'division of the season', the Japanese 'Setsubun' is the day before the commencement of each season. In common usage, Setsubun is generally accepted as the term for the spring Setsubun, correctly known as Risshun, and celebrated every 3 February.

Throughout Japanese homes you will hear *'Oni wa saoto! Fuku wa uchi!'* being projected in a loud voice by the head of each family: literally translated this means 'Demons Out! Luck In!' and is traditionally accompanied by the throwing of heated soya beans out of the front door onto the street. The act of throwing the beans is thought to purify the home and cast out evil and is derived from a famous Buddhist monk who, in the Heian era (794-1185 AD), exorcised an evil spirit by throwing beans out of his house.

Priests at both Shinto and Buddhist temples throughout Japan throw beans in a public display of ceremony on Setsubun, while guests will be invited to throw beans wrapped in coloured foils. Sweets and treats are also cast into the audiences, who gather at shrines for the festivities, and often celebrities will be involved – continuing the tradition of Setsubun.

In smaller displays it is customary for families to decorate the entrances to their homes with holly and fish-heads in the hope that the spiky plant and unpleasant-smelling head will ward off evil forces who might otherwise try to enter. Family elders will eat a bean for each year of their age, plus one extra to ensure good luck will befall them in the coming year.

RIGHT: *Shinto temples are awash with beans during Setsubun, as this action is thought to dispel demons.*

OSTARA

SPRING EQUINOX AND WITCHES' LESSER SABBAT
21 March

Celebrated on the spring equinox, Ostara, named after the Anglo-Saxon goddess of spring, Eostre, is an ancient festival of rebirth. It celebrates the return of the goddess's consort following his winter retreat into the Land of the Dead.

The egg is the symbol of this feast day for a variety of reasons. It is a universal symbol of renewal and new life, bringing with it hope and promise of the future. In direct terms, the egg was associated with Ostara because it was the time of year when hens would begin laying eggs – bringing food and sustenance. Chickens only lay eggs during times of the year when at least 12 hours of sun hits the retinas of their eyes, despite the ancients' attempts to fool them by placing them alongside bright fires. Eggs would only be laid between the spring and autumn equinoxes.

The Christian word 'Easter' is derived from the name of the ancient goddess Eostre. The popular symbol of modern-day Easter, the Easter Bunny, is clearly a character derived from the Eostre Hare.

Legend has it that all the animals in the woodland loved Eostre, and at the spring equinox they would gather gifts to offer her. One of her devotees was a young hare who wished to find

BELOW: *A mystical rite takes place during the ancient festival of Ostara to welcome the goddess's consort back home.*

a special gift for Eostre but knowing her to be powerful and able to obtain anything she wished for he was confused about what he could possibly give that would be of any value to her. One day he came across a beautiful fresh egg while foraging in the vegetation and he was just about to break it open when he thought of Eostre. Perhaps this would make a perfect gift for her? After some pondering, he realized that she would probably have all the eggs she could ever need and so, tucking the egg carefully under his arm, he returned home. Later that evening he wondered how he might make the egg special so that it would reflect the beauty that Eostre brought to the world each spring. He began decorating the shell with colourful paints made from the flowers in the forest, and drew symbols of Eostre all over the egg. When he had finished he bounded through the forest in search of the goddess and presented her with his decorated egg. Eostre was so pleased with his gift that she wanted all children, themselves representative of new life, throughout the world to enjoy the same treat. Thus the tale of the Easter Bunny delivering decorated eggs was born. The tale of course has been largely forgotten and the careful decoration replaced with gaudy silver foils and mass-manufactured chocolate sweets, but the principle remains the same.

The egg-decorating custom came originally from the Teutonic traditions

ABOVE: *A young maiden accompanies a rabbit into the forest during Ostara, an ancient echo of today's tradition of the Easter-egg hunt.*

in which Eostre was first worshipped, but it is commonly reported, incorrectly, that it began in America in 1862 when First Lady Dolly Madison hosted an 'egg roll' on the lawns of the Capitol Building in Washington DC. President Abraham Lincoln was the next American to tap into the universal symbolism of the egg when he ordered decorated eggs and treats to be hidden around the gardens of the White House and invited children to search for them on Easter morning. But the first Easter-egg hunts began 2,000 years earlier in Asia where the discovery of an egg represented finding a life renewed. The rise of Christianity in Europe drove Pagan customs 'underground', and the offering of eggs to the goddess at the spring equinox had to be hidden – another reference to the Easter-egg hunts that are enjoyed worldwide today.

WALPURGIS NIGHT
30 April (May Day's Eve)

Walpurgis Night, celebrated with gusto on May Day's Eve in Germany, Finland, Sweden, Romania and the Czech Republic, derives its name from St Walburga, niece of St Boniface and according to legend, daughter of St Richard, a Saxon prince. She became a nun in the German convent of Heidenheim, which was founded by Brother Wunibald. She passed from this life on 25 February 779, and on 1 May of the same year she was sainted.

Celebrations of Walpurgis Night, or *Walpurgisnacht* as it is known in Germany, originate from early Pagan customs, which honoured the return of life to the earth with the coming of spring. Bonfires would be lit to mark the turn of the season and it was believed that witches would gather to hold a sabbat on Brocken Mountain – the highest peak in the Harz Mountains – to await signs of the arrival of spring.

Now to the Brocken the witches ride;
The stubble is gold and the corn is green;
There is the carnival crew to be seen,
And Squire Urianus will come to preside.
So over the valleys our company floats,
with witches a-farting on stinking old goats.
Excerpt from Goethe's *Faust*

In Viking history, celebrations of fertility took place at the end of April, and as they spread throughout Europe these two celebrations – the Viking and the German – were amalgamated to create the festival still held today.

In Swedish culture, the celebration of Walpurgis Night (known as Valborg) has become as important as Christmas and is marked with song and the lighting of fires. Historically, it was customary for children to collect greenery and branches to decorate the homes of their families, for which they would be paid in eggs. Since 1909, a grand carnival parade has been held in Gothenburg each Walpurgis Night, during which copious amounts of alcohol are consumed and a wild night is had by all.

In the Czech Republic, grass or sand is placed over the threshold of homes in the belief that witches have to count each blade of grass or grain of sand before entering. It is also believed that if you stick a pitchfork in the ground with the prongs upward you might catch a witch as she flies by.

BELOW: *Spiritual forces are said to celebrate the 'Walpurgisnacht', as it is known in Germany, every year on 30 April.*

BELTHANE

FIRE FESTIVAL AND WITCHES' GREATER SABBAT
1 May

BELOW: *Balefires are lit on Belthane to ensure plentiful crop growth in the coming season.*

Belthane, or 'Bright Fire, is an ancient Celtic fire festival that has its roots in many cultures. Celebrations on 1 May were instigated originally to welcome back the heat of the sun – generally regarded as male in Pagan belief – to ensure good crops throughout the coming season. Libations were offered to the gods, sometimes in the form of human or animal sacrifice, and merry-making was enjoyed in the shape of feasting, dancing and procreating.

In Scotland, 'balefires' would be lit upon every hill to quicken the seeds in the ground with their warmth and to drive away disease from cattle. Celebrants would take turns jumping through the fire and driving cattle among the flames in a belief that this would ensure their continued wellbeing for the coming year. Balefire ashes were often kept in a bag and worn as a fertility charm around the neck or strewn on fields to aid the growth of new crops. Marking the first day of summer in the Celtic calendar, Belthane is thought to be named after the Pagan god Bel, or Belenus, who is called upon and welcomed as the 'Horned God' in heathen celebrations.

Traces of festivals at this time of year can be found in Rome, where sacred statuary known as 'The Herms' would be erected in wood or stone at crossroads and decorated with greenery on 1 May. With the arrival of the Romans in Britain and the resulting amalgamation of Roman and Celtic traditions, Belthane became one of the most important of the fire festivals in the calendar.

Traditions at Belthane include erecting a maypole, which is still continued in some parts of rural England. The pole is crowned with garlands, flowers and branches in an offering to the Roman goddesses Flora and Maia (after whom the month of May gets its name), while colourful ribbons or streamers hang at its side awaiting the commencement of the maypole dance. During the ritual dance equal numbers of males and females entwine the ribbons in an elaborate fashion to plait and decorate the pole. It is thought this custom has its roots in Druid tree customs, which were carried out to ensure fertility of the land, and therefore an abundance of vegetables and flowers throughout the summer.

The symbol of the Green Man is very much associated with Belthane and in times past a male villager would dress in the leaves of the forest and bring back branches and shoots to decorate the village, thus symbolizing the return of the god figure in an abundant form. Other villagers would dress as the May Queen and King, symbolising the new union of god and goddess at this time of year. The theme of fertility is most potent in the Pagan calendar at Belthane with sexual union high on the agenda for those enjoying the festivities. Food was consumed in large quantities as the joyous summer came back into the lives of those who celebrated the festival of Belthane.

LEMURIA
9–13 May

In Rome, 'The Lemures' have been celebrated and feared day and night from 9–13 May each year since ancient times. It is believed that the unhappy wraiths of those who were improperly buried or whose graves have been neglected since death will rise to terrorize the living. At midnight they are said to drag their wretched souls from their graves and rise to walk in the land of the sentient, hell-bent on wreaking havoc and death.

Referred to as 'Lemuria', the entire month of May is considered an inauspicious time to plan events such as weddings or celebrations, with the belief that they might be wrecked by the angered spirits who are around. In times past, all plans for joyous occasions were held off until June when the ghosts were said to be in a more ambivalent frame of mind.

ABOVE: *The unquiet spirits of ancient Rome venture forth from their tombs during the festival of Lemuria.*

OPPOSITE BOTTOM: *A Belthane custom is enacted inside a magic circle.*

LITHA

THE MIDSUMMER SOLSTICE: SOLSTICE AND WITCHES' GREATER SABBAT
21 June

Shakespeare did a wonderful job of encompassing all that Litha – the midsummer solstice – is all about in his work *A Midsummer Night's Dream*, where faeries, magic and mischief abound on one bewitched night in the forest.

The word 'solstice' means literally 'sun stands still' and midsummer, called Litha by modern Pagans, is a celebration of the longest day, when the power of the sun, represented as the male aspect of deity, is at his strongest. The date for this festival, as with all Celtic celebrations, varies from source to source – but the symbolic significance of what it represents is always the same.

In the past it was believed that the power of the faerie world was at its strongest on midsummer's eve and that a doorway between worlds would open on this magical night for those that sought it. Plants and herbs would be gathered, the belief being that this was the most potent time for their hidden medicinal or magical properties. In some cultures bonfires were lit to scare away the presence of the dark faerie who might try and create mischief in the land of the living. Perhaps the best known modern day celebrations of the midsummer solstice occur at Stonehenge in Wiltshire where each year thousands of followers of old faiths are given free access to join in celebrating the power of the sun.

The standing stones, or monoliths, at Stonehenge are perfectly aligned so that they mark the position of the rising sun at the midsummer solstice. As the sun rises over the heel stone it casts a long phallic shadow into the heart of the circle itself, thereby representing the marriage and sexual unity of the Sun God (male) and Earth Mother (female).

The origin of the name 'Litha' is unknown; some think that it may be an Anglo-Saxon word, although there is little evidence for this. Others take the word to have some opposite meaning to 'Yule', which is exactly six months away on the opposite side of the Wheel of the Year.

RIGHT: *The power of the sun is celebrated at Litha. Here a showman celebrates its power with a fire dance.*

OPPOSITE TOP: *Corn from fields is baked into a celebratory loaf at 'Loaf Mass' every first day in August.*

OPPOSITE BOTTOM: *Ancient lanterns are illuminated at the end of the Obon festival to help guide ancestors back to the land of the dead.*

LUGHNASADH

FIRE FESTIVAL AND WITCHES' LESSER SABBAT
1 August

In Gaelic history, Lughnasadh, meaning 'Festival of Lugh' (the Sun God), was one of the four main festivals on the medieval Irish calendar. Also known as Lammas, the first of three harvest festivals – the others being Mabon and Samhain (Hallowe'en) – it is believed to have its origins in Anglo-Saxon England. Lammas means 'Loaf Mass' and is the time of the year when thanks is given to the spiritual forces around us for the plentiful bounty of the summer months. Traditionally the first baked loaf was offered to the god and goddess as thanks for their gifts of crops and sunshine.

The original celebration was a commemoration of the death of the Corn God, sometimes known as John Barleycorn. Followers of old faiths, including Paganism, would make a loaf in the shape of the Corn God, which they would subsequently sacrifice and eat. The symbolism of this act shows the gift from the Sun God of the corn, which is reaped (dies), and made into flour and then loaves (to be eaten). The last sheaf of corn is never ground for flour and is brought into the home where it is fashioned into the shape of the god and kept hidden safely away – to ensure the return of the god in the coming year.

Modern Paganism celebrates this festival with harvesting, cooking and feasting – a time for enjoying the fruits of your labour. It is also a time when, traditionally, hand-fasting would take place. Hand-fasting is a type of Pagan wedding ceremony in which partners live together for 12 months to see if they are happy together, before committing for life at the next Lughnasadh, or parting company.

OBON
13–15 July

The joyous festival of Obon, celebrated in Japan each year, is a Buddhist event with its main focus on commemorating one's ancestors. Held annually for three days, it is recognized as one of Japan's major holiday seasons with an influx of travel, spending and tourism being noted at this time of year.

Brightly coloured lanterns filled with votive candles are hung to shimmer in the breeze – a guiding light to welcome back the ancestral spirits into their former homes. Inside, small shrines to the deceased are erected and decorated with the favourite foods and drinks of those relatives who have passed on. Rather than being a sombre affair, Obon is a joyous time of welcoming back those we love into the embrace of the family for a short while.

After the festival is over, the lanterns that helped the spirits find their way back to their former homes are cast into a river or lake and gently guide the ghosts back to their land of the dead – until next Obon, when they will return once more.

MABON

AUTUMN EQUINOX AND WITCHES' LESSER SABBAT
21 September

Tracing the origins of this second of the three harvest festivals is not easy. It seems from most sources that it is a modern creation by the neo-Pagan movement of America, although some references in Anglo-Saxon history do indicate that a sacred festival took place at this time of the year.

The word 'equinox' comes form the Latin word *aequinoctium* meaning 'equal night', and on the autumn equinox balance is a central theme to the festival, as at this time of year days and nights are the same length. It is a season of abundant harvest and thanksgiving.

The term 'Mabon' derives from a Welsh god-figure and was used in the 1970s by Aidan Kelly as a Wiccan name for the autumn equinox. It is more commonly used in the USA where the rise in popularity of Paganism, witchcraft and alternative faith systems has led to a boom in book publishing on these topics, thereby spreading the use of the term. In the UK, many Pagans and witches refuse to use the name, calling the festival simply 'the autumn equinox' or by the Druidic name Aban Efed. Whatever you call it, Mabon is rooted firmly within the celebrations of ancient forces believed to be responsible for the crops harvested at this time of year.

In the fields, corn was reaped, while in cottage gardens fresh vegetables were unearthed, and in orchards ripe fruit was plucked from the trees. Although Mabon is a celebration of plenty, a cornucopia of thanksgiving to the god and goddess, restraint is also implied – much of the food must be stored for the cold and bitter months to come. As well as being termed 'the witches' thanksgiving', Mabon is also the first day of autumn, when the wind begins to whip up the leaves and the nights draw in.

In various cultures a particular goddess was remembered at Mabon – the Goddess of the Grain. She has various names in different countries but in Greece she was Demeter, the Spirit of the Grain. Her child was represented by the seeds that fell to the ground from the mother grain-plant; these would then be sown for the following year's crop next spring. The manifestation of Demeter was seen as the abundant crop of the current year, while her daughter, Persephone, was the seed for the year to come.

SAMHAIN
FIRE FESTIVAL AND WITCHES' GREATER SABBAT
31 October

The best known and most celebrated festival of the haunted world is undoubtedly Hallowe'en, or Samhain, to give it the Celtic name. Although Hallowe'en has, more recently, become a commercial opportunity to launch the latest horror movie, and a time when children dress up in costume and go door to door in their neighborhood asking for sweets, it is in fact an ancient custom which has its roots in the culture of the British Isles.

In the Celtic calendar, Samhain was the last night of the year, with 1 November being the first day of the New Year, and this was, consequently, a time of great celebration – a time for looking back at the past and planning for the new year to come. It was believed that the spirits of ancestors would return temporarily to the living world for one night of communion with the sentient. In the same way that Hallowe'en was 'between times' – halfway between the harvest festival of Mabon and the winter solstice of Yule – people believed that the rift between our world and that of the dead was at its most vulnerable on this special night, and would lay down offerings of food and drink for those who may be revisiting their old haunts.

The commonly used term 'Hallowe'en' derived from the earlier names of 'All Hallows Eve' and 'All Hallow Even', both Christianized versions of the original Celtic celebration that had been demonized by the Church. By naming 1 November 'All Hallows Day' and 2 November 'All Souls Day', the Christian church attempted to blot

ABOVE: *The witch – seen here in a rather comical pose – is prevalent at Hallowe'en, the last day of the Celtic year.*

out the ancient customs, believing them, then, to be a form of devil worship. (In actual fact Pagans do not believe in the Devil – he is a concept created by the Christian faith itself.)

On Hallowe'en it was customary for villagers to light enormous bonfires and throw upon them the bones of cattle who had perished. This is where the term 'bonfire' is derived from; it was originally 'bone fire'. Before the fire was lit it was ensured that all the hearths in the village were cold, and after the bone fire was blazing each would take a part of the fire to light their own, thereby uniting the villagers on this special eve.

Hallowe'en was then largely forgotten, and it wasn't until a resurgence of interest in ancient beliefs began to resurface in the 1960s that Hallowe'en began to be celebrated again. This happened primarily in the USA, though the concept has now crept back to the British Isles, where it began, with Hallowe'en parties, costumes and themed products now widely accepted.

Traditional activities at Hallowe'en include the creation of hideous jack-o'-lanterns, originally carved turnips with gruesome faces lit by a solitary candle. The availability of pumpkins in the USA meant that the tradition changed vegetable – pumpkins being larger and easier to carve. Rather than being designed to frighten people, as is commonly thought, the Hallowe'en faces glowing from darkened windows were originally intended as a deterrent to mischievous spirits intent on bringing harm or trouble to the home.

Hallowe'en is also a time for spell-making and divination, with modern witches harnessing its potent power for their magic. Fortune-telling is also popular on this eve; with the connection to the spirit world stronger than at any other time of the year, it is believed possible to ask any question and receive an answer. Unmarried females also play a game at the stroke of midnight – by staring intently at their own eyes in a mirror by the light of a single candle, they hope to see a vision of their husband-to-be. Other games include bobbing for apples in a pail of water using your teeth, and trying to bite a doughnut from a piece of string without using your hands.

Many dread the sound of knocking at their front door on this night, for it is the time when 'trick or treating' takes place. Dressed as a ghost, witch or other horror, children and teenagers step into the gloom of the night to collect sweets and money from neighbours and friends. This custom evolved from Mischief Night – another name for Hallowe'en – where it was believed that naughty spirits would upset your home unless placated with offerings of sweet foods or treasures.

THE DAYS OF THE DEAD
1–2 November

Known locally as *Los Dias de Los Muertos* (The Days of the Dead), this Mexican festival is a cornucopia of colourful celebration, which honours the deceased in both urban and rural areas across the country each year. Celebrated with great enthusiasm each 1 and 2 November, the precise heritage of the festival is complex, but is believed to be the result of a mixture of pre-Hispanic and Catholic rituals and beliefs.

The roots of this world-famous festival, which attracts visitors from all over the globe, extend back to the 8th century when the Church declared 1 November 'All Saint's day'. This 24-hour vigil, intended to honour the Catholic martyrs and saints, was an attempt to replace an existing tradition instigated by the Celts some 2,000 years earlier. The Celts and their Druidic priests had long marked the turn of the New Year on 1 November, celebrating through lighting fires, feasting and merry-making. They believed that the veil between our world and the spirit world was at its weakest at this time of year, and as we have seen, they welcomed back the spirits of the past on the day they named Samhain (see p.71) – to join with the living in their revelry. Today, the activities and customs practised throughout Mexico are a mix of early Celtic traditions, Roman Catholic overlay and Spanish, Aztec and Mayan influences, which have combined to create what is now a national public holiday.

In the weeks leading up to the celebration, shops and markets are bedecked with colourful decorations, sweets and food, which are used in homes to honour the dead and remember family ancestors. Candies in the shape of skulls and coffins glare ominously at hungry children peering in shop windows, while wreaths of black silk flowers are hung on market-traders' stalls.

BELOW: *Papier mâché models bedeck shop windows, home altars and parades to honour the dead as part of* Los Dias de Los Muertos, *the festival known as The Days of the Dead.*

Families collect items which belonged to their loved ones who have passed to the spirit world and display these on commemorative altars which are temporarily constructed in their homes. These are likely to include photographs and offerings in the shape of specially baked bread called *animas* – believed to represent the soul of the spirits they are honouring. No expense is spared with the commemorative shrine, which is usually constructed on top of three levels of empty upturned boxes covered with a white cloth. Four candles are placed at the top of the altar to represent the cardinal directions of North, South, East and West, and subsequent candles inscribed with the names of those gone before are placed in prime positions. Brightly coloured flowers and decorated candles are added to welcome the spirits on the Day of the Dead, when it is believed they will return to our world for 24 hours to share memories, tears and laughter. The offerings of food and water are given to quench the hunger and thirst of the spirits after their long journey to our land from the world of the dead, and other luxuries which they might have enjoyed in life might also be placed on the altar, such as tobacco, beer and wine. A special incense made from the resin of the copal tree is burned to attract the spirits and draw them home. It is also used to cleanse the house and ward off evil. It is usual to see a basin of fresh water, soap, towel and comb placed near to the altar – to allow the spirits to refresh themselves after their journey, before joining the feast in their honour.

On 1 November, the spirits of Mexico's lost children are remembered with gusto and their graves are decorated with paper streamers, toys and candy. On the following day it is the turn of the adults, and families gather in gravesites where they hold lavish picnics while toasting the graves of those who have left the mortal plane. At this time of year gravestones and monuments are spruced up, weeds are pulled from the ground and beautiful flowers are laid around each memorial – most notably marigolds which are known in Mexico as 'Flowers of The Dead'. Later, as darkness falls, tombs and family burial sites light up the sky as thousands of votive candles illuminate the sepulchres – lighting the way for the dead to return at midnight.

Los Dias de Los Muertos plays a major role in Mexican heritage and belief – it rejoices in death and sees it not as an end, but as an evolution of the spirit; a natural transition in life which should not be feared. Despite the modern onslaught of America's 'Hallowe'en', which is now beginning to blend with the customs of the Mexican festival, its roots are firmly planted in this eclectic people, as visitors to_ this colourful spectacle can so easily observe, and it is unlikely that it will ever be forgotten.

BELOW: *The outwardly morbid image of a skeleton is decorated and adorned to welcome back memories of past ancestors.*

YULE

THE MIDWINTER SOLSTICE AND WITCHES' LESSER SABBAT
21 December

Yule, or Yuletide as it is often referred to, is the name for the winter solstice, a wonderful festival of hope while in the grip of winter. A time for feasting and dance, the word Yule is thought to mean 'Feast of The Wheel' – a nod to the 'Wheel of the Year' recognized in many older traditions and belief systems, most notably Paganism. In the middle of winter the 'Wheel' is slowed and ready to begin turning again toward the summer, bringing new life and hope in the difficult struggle that is winter.

Yule celebrations pre-date Christianity and many of the traditions associated with the Christian festival of Christmas have their origin in Yule. The sacrifice of a pig to the god Freyr in Scandinavia at Yule has now become the tradition of the 'Christmas Ham' which sits on Christmas feast tables throughout the world. The 'Yule Log' – now thought of as a delicious chocolate confection stuffed with cream – was actually a real log which would be thrown onto the Yule fire in order that revellers would watch it burn and remember that the sun was coming back to the world. At the end of the fire a piece of the log would be taken from the embers and kept safely until the next year when a new Yule log would be lit by the remains of its forefather. The traditions of hanging holly and mistletoe in the home also have their basis in Pagan celebration. The mistletoe represented the seed of the god and was thus a potent fertility symbol under which partners would kiss, and thus be blessed with fertility for the coming summer. Holly is welcomed into the home as it represents the Holly King – another aspect of male deity.

ABOVE: *The winter solstice is celebrated in earnest at Stonehenge by contemporary Pagans, witches and Druids.*

When the first Christian missionaries began suppressing older faith systems in Europe, they found it easier to create new meanings for existing festivals, such as Yule, instead of trying to stamp them out. Thus Christmas was inaugurated, adopting many of the traditions of Yule.

In neo-Pagan practice the observance and celebration of Yule is of great importance, being one of the four major sabbats within the Wheel of the Year. It is observed in a manner that commemorates the death of the Holly King – symbolizing the old year and shortened sun, at the hands of his son and successor the Oak King – symbolizing the new sun that is gaining each day. In nature the wren is seen as the old year who now retires, while the robin redbreast comes to the fore, bringing with him the power of the sun god.

LEFT: *In the grip of winter, 'Yule' is celebrated to welcome back the power of the sun – symbolizing hope for the future.*

BELOW: *A traditional solstice scene, depicting a 'wise woman' and a witch's cauldron on a blazing fire.*

YUE LAN
Every 14th day of the seventh Full Moon

In China, the dead rise again on the 14th day of the seventh Full Moon, when Yue Lan is observed. In this spooky festival of the dead, similar to the Roman Lemuria, it is believed that those who were murdered, lost at sea or have no families to remember them return to our world intent on disruption. The festival is held to keep spirits up, so to speak! While the gates of the underworld are open for one night of the Chinese calendar, it is said that the ghosts of those long dead are 'hungry' for the living, and thus the name 'Festival of the Hungry Ghosts' was born.

The most elaborate part of this festival is the creation of the intricate paper models which are fashioned in the shape of worldly possessions such as household goods, luxuries and even money – known as 'Hell Notes', which are only valid in the eerie underworld of Yinjian, the world of darkness. The models and money adorn beaches, gravesites and streets in the hope that they will appease the hungry ghosts and leave the living in peace.

In temples, a special crown with gold and red symbols depicting the most powerful hungry ghosts is worn by the priest who stands before an altar of offerings brought by locals. This might include bread, cakes and sweet treats. The priest will perform a ceremony which is supposed to increase the quantity of food and then, after three hours of chanting and blessing, the offering is set alight in a mighty blaze and sent off to the spirit world. In this strange spectacular the ghosts are sent back to their world, their hunger appeased for the year.

BELOW: *Vast quantities of food are set alight in the culmination of the 'Festival of the Hungry Ghosts'. The food is sent via smoke to the spirit land in order to appease the wraiths.*

Chapter 3
The History of Spirit Photography

Since the invention of the camera, man has tried to capture the definitive evidence to prove the existence of ghosts on film. To many this was achieved in 1936 with the most famous ghost photograph of all – The Brown Lady of Raynham Hall. To others the 'evidence' of ghost photography is nothing more than a trick of the light, misinterpretation of the image or in some cases deliberate fraud.

In the heyday of Victorian spiritualism, the scope for faking 'ghosts' on film was vast. Thousands of 'spirit extras' manifested on photographs, with customers paying high sums to have a 'picture with the dead'. Some faked images are ridiculous in the extreme – take the example of Helen Duncan, a famous medium from the 1930s. One of the most reproduced pictures of a spirit manifestation, there appears to be a ghost exuding from her face in the form of an ectoplasmic humanoid form. It is clearly a not-so-elaborate deception, involving a badly painted papier-mâché mask draped in an old sheet; but at the time it was accepted.

Some photographs were more elaborate, with multiple images being laid on top of each other. The first fake ghost photographs were created by William Mumler in 1861. He was an engraver by trade and lived in Boston, USA. His sideline in phantom fakery began when he started taking pictures of his customers in which faint faces appeared. Business boomed until it was realized that the faces were actually those of living residents of Boston which he had over-printed to achieve the ghostly effects. He was arrested and charged with fraud.

Some pictures, however, have stood the test of time. They have been analysed by generations of researchers for signs of tampering or deliberate fakery. As we move into a digital age the potential for mistrusting images we are presented with increases. Let us take a fresh look at some of the most enduring images of what are believed to be genuine ghost photographs captured throughout the ages.

CONTEMPORARY GHOST PHOTOGRAPHY
Globes of Light

Often referred to as 'orbs', these small discs of light have been appearing in force since digital cameras became widely available in the late 1990s. Believers explain them as a form of ghostly energy. Sceptics, on the other hand, are more likely to dismiss them as the result of dust or moisture particles which, when caught in the light of a camera flash, appear to have three-dimensional form.

After spending some years investigating the phenomena of 'orbs', it is my conclusion that in almost all cases they are not of paranormal origin. However, I have been in the presence of people at the very time that they have seen these alluring globes of light with the naked eye, moving in a strange fashion as if to indicate intelligent understanding of what is being said to them. In these instances it is more difficult to blame digital cameras and explain them away.

Misty Forms

Appearing mostly as a blue/grey smoky substance, these relatively common types of ghost photograph have replaced the Victorian cheesecloth (which fraudsters used to chew up and hide in their mouths, to then regurgitate) as the modern-day version of 'ectoplasm'. Sometimes interpreted as humanoid forms, faces or animals, those with a believing

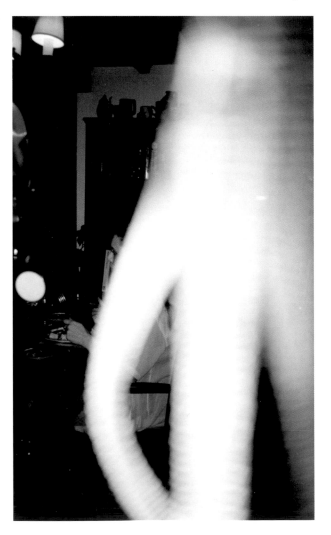

eye explain that these are the partially formed appearance of spirits. Others say they can create the same effect by blowing cigarette smoke in front of a camera and then taking a picture. An alternative explanation is that the mist is formed by the photographer's breath on cold days.

After examining hundreds of this type of image and capturing several examples myself I find them hard to fully explain. On various occasions I have caught this kind of picture when no-one has been smoking in the vicinity and the weather has been mild.

Vortices

The haunted world is divided when it comes to pictures of glowing spirals of light. On one side sit those who say they are simply the strap of the camera obscuring the lens, while on the other side there are those who explain these vortex-like images as an invisible energy form which is the beginning of a ghost taking human form.

It is easy to replicate this kind of image by placing a camera strap or similar in front of a camera lens and taking a picture – I have tried this and the result matches many of the vortex pictures believed to be ghostly manifestations. What are not so easy to understand, though, are photographs taken on occasions when no strap was in evidence and the camera was not obscured by any normal physical means.

A good example of a striking vortex was captured by myself in a very old house I grew up in. I sent it to leading ghost-photographer Maurice Grosse, who was unable to offer any kind of explanation for it and it remains a mystery. Incidentally the house was haunted, and some have commented on the vaguely humanoid form created by the three fronds and the 'head'.

RIGHT: *This 'orb' was photographed at St Werburgh's Church in Derby by members of The Ghost Research Foundation International. Its characteristics – including the three-dimensional appearance, central 'nucleus' and outer rim – are often used by believers to vouch for its authenticity.*

BELOW: *Taken in the grounds of Alston Hall, Birmingham, this strange ectoplasmic form was not seen at the time of exposure and appears to be hovering between the photographer and his subject – the woman in the red coat.*

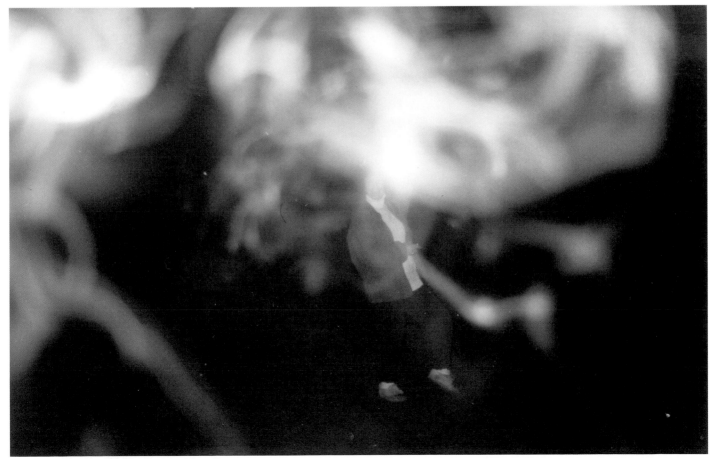

THE BROWN LADY OF RAYNHAM HALL

19 September 1936

BELOW: *A portrait of Dorothy Walpole, thought to be Raynham Hall's 'Brown Lady'. Plagued by mental illness, Dorothy led an unhappy life, and her quiet yet slightly menacing ghost has reminded past visitors of this fact.*

The undisputed queen of ghostly images has to be the enigmatic, perfect image of Raynham Hall's 'Brown Lady'. Taken by two unsuspecting photographers from *Country Life* magazine in 1936 the image has withstood over 80 years of analysis and remains the best example of a ghost on film to this day.

Seventeenth-century Raynham Hall is the country seat of the Townsend family and sightings of the 'Brown Lady' pre-date the photograph by more than a century. It is thought that the ghost is the restless shade of Dorothy Walpole, a direct blood-relative of the Townsends who lived unhappily at the Hall – she suffered from mental illness and was confined to an oak-panelled bedroom where her portrait still hangs. After her children were taken from her Dorothy either fell, or was pushed, down the grand staircase to her death, and her spirit has walked the hallways and staircase at Raynham ever since. Her apparition is often silent and harmless but on occasions a feeling of menacing evil has accompanied her manifestation, the most celebrated of which was in 1835.

Captain Frederick Marryat, a British Naval Captain, came to Raynham as a guest of Lord and Lady Charles Townsend. He was shown to a bedroom on the first floor in which the painting of Dorothy Walpole hung, her sad forlorn face staring at him from the confines of the picture frame. As a precaution he placed a loaded revolver beneath his pillow before he went to sleep, but it seemed it would not be needed, as the first two nights passed without event. On the third night he had cause to venture to another room at the other end of the Hall: to meet with Lord Townsend's nephews who had expressed an interest in his opinion of a new gun one of them had bought. By the light of a candle, and carrying his revolver, he left his bedroom and walked along the corridor. After some convivial discussion concerning the new gun, Marryat and the boys made their way out into the corridor where they were amazed to see a floating figure of a woman emerge from Captain Marryat's bed chamber. She was dressed in a gown of brown satin which rustled as she moved and she had a ruff around her throat. Terrified, Captain Marryat shot at the ghost, the sound piercing the silence and smoke from the gun obscuring their view. When the smoke cleared there was nothing to be seen, other than a bullet firmly lodged in the wood panelling.

News of this celebrated sighting and the dramatic tale of Captain Marryat attempting to 'shoot' a ghost soon spread throughout the neighbourhood. Combined with other ghostly tales at Raynham – including alleged sightings of a phantom horse, a pink lady, a cavalier dressed in red and the phantom forms of two children it created such hysteria that in 1849 the entire staff at the Hall walked out *en masse*! The next publicised sighting came to light in 1926 when the then Lady Townsend admitted that her son and his friend had watched the ghost on the staircase and had identified it with the portrait hanging in the haunted bedroom.

The photograph which has made this case so prominent in the paranormal world was caught by chance at 4pm on 19 September 1936. Lady Townsend had invited the popular magazine *Country Life* to publish a feature on the house and grounds and after taking copious shots of the glorious gardens, photographer Captain Provand and his assistant Indre

Shira had set up their camera and flash at the bottom of the grand oak staircase – haunt of the Brown Lady. Indre Shira described what happened next in the issue of *Country Life* dated 26 December 1936:

'Captain Provand took one photograph of it while I flashed the light. He was focussing again for another exposure; I was standing by his side just behind the camera with the flashlight pistol in my hand, looking directly up the staircase. All at once I detected an ethereal, veiled form coming slowly down the stairs. Rather excitedly I called out sharply: 'Quick! Quick! There's something! Are you ready?' 'Yes' the photographer replied, and removed the cap from the lens. I pressed the trigger of the flashlight pistol. After the flash, and on closing the shutter, Captain Provand removed the focussing cloth from his head and, turning to me, said: 'What's all the excitement about?' I directed his attention to the staircase and explained that I had distinctly seen a figure there – transparent so that the steps were visible through the ethereal form, but nevertheless very definite and to me perfectly real. He laughed and said I must have imagined I had seen a ghost – for there was nothing now to be seen. It may be of interest to record that the flash from the Sasha bulb, which in this instance was used, is equivalent, I

ABOVE: *Perhaps the most famous of all ghost photographs, the 'Brown Lady' was snapped by a photographer from* Country Life *magazine in 1936 after she was seen floating down the staircase. It has never been proved a fake and remains the best example of a genuine ghost photograph in existence.*

Raynham Hall East

ABOVE: *A photograph of Raynham Hall taken in 1906 shows an eastern view of the building.*

understand, to a speed of one-fiftieth part of a second. After securing several other pictures, we decided to pack up and return to Town. Nearly all the way back we were arguing about the possibility of obtaining a genuine ghost photograph. Captain Provand laid down the law most emphatically by assuring me that as a Court photographer of 30 years' standing, it was quite impossible to obtain an authentic ghost photograph – unless, possibly, in a séance room – and in that connection he had had no experience. I have neither his technical skill nor long years of practical experience as a portraitist, neither am I interested in psychic phenomena; but I maintained that the form of a very refined influence was so real to my eyes that it must have been caught at that psychological moment by the lens of the camera…

When the negatives of Raynham Hall were developed, I stood beside Captain Provand in the dark-room. One after the other they were placed in the developer. Suddenly Captain Provand exclaimed: 'Good Lord! There's something on the staircase negative, after all!' I took one glance, called to him 'Hold it' and dashed downstairs to the chemist, Mr Benjamin Jones, manager of Blake, Sandford and Blake, whose premises are immediately underneath our studio. I invited Mr Jones to come upstairs to our dark-room. He came, and saw the negative just as it had been taken from the developer and placed in the adjoining hypo bath. Afterwards, he declared that, had he not seen for himself the negative being fixed, he would not have believed in the genuineness of the picture. Incidentally, Mr Jones had considerable experience as an amateur photographer in developing his own plates and films. Mr Jones, Captain Provand and I vouch for the fact that the negative has not been retouched in any way. It has been examined critically by a number of experts. No one can account for the appearance of the ghostly figure; but it is there, clear enough.'

THE GIRL IN THE FIRE

19 November 1995

Captured by local town resident Tony O'Rahilly, this image of Wem Town Hall in Shropshire during a fire on 19 November 1995 clearly shows a young girl staring around the edge of a doorway amidst the blaze. The girl was not witnessed at the time of exposure and would clearly not be standing in such a composed state if she were a sentient being. She could only have been unaffected by the intense heat if she was a ghost, and this is one argument for the authentication of this particular ghost photograph.

The picture was passed to the Association for the Scientific Study of Anomalous Phenomena (ASSAP) who in turn passed it to Dr Vernon Harrison, a photographic expert and former president of the Royal Photographic Society. Neither ASSAP nor Dr Harrison believed the picture to have been tampered with or manipulated and both said it appeared to be genuine.

Some intriguing speculation has added a further dimension to this story, connecting this fire to another fire in Wem, dating back to 1677. The fire devastated the town, levelling many of the wood-constructed buildings of the time. It was blamed on a young serving girl named Jane Chum who accidentally set fire to the thatched roof of her home with a candle. Her ghost is well known throughout the town and there are still sporadic sightings of her wraith – always carrying a candle. Many of Wem's contemporary residents believe that this picture, taken in 1995, shows her ghost.

BELOW: *A ghostly face stares out from the burning remains of Wem Town Hall; her appearance remains unexplained.*

RIGHT: *This strange and rather outdated looking lady, perched atop a tombstone at Bachelor's Grove Cemetery, was caught at the same time as ghost hunters' equipment was registering strange fluctuations.*

OPPOSITE TOP: *Lord Combermere seems to be sitting in his favourite chair in this photograph from 1891, yet his body was being buried some four miles away at the time.*

OPPOSITE BOTTOM: *The ghosts of The Queen's House, Greenwich, remain unexplained despite attempts to communicate with them via a séance in 1967 by The Ghost Club Society.*

THE WOMAN IN THE GRAVEYARD
10 August 1991

This remarkable photograph showing an apparently three-dimensional woman perching atop a gravestone was captured by The Ghost Research Society of America, run by well-known investigator Dale Kaczmarek. The image was snapped by Ghost Research Society member Jude Huff-Felz at the same time that inexplicable readings were observed on the ghost hunters' equipment, although the woman was not seen at the time. The clothing worn by the ghostly woman has been described as 'out of date', adding credence to the picture, which has been published in numerous books and media throughout the world. Bachelor's Grove Cemetery in Chicago, where the photograph was taken, has a long reputation for being haunted. It is a small remote collection of gravestones surrounded by a metal fence and is somewhat neglected. There are said to be over 100 reports of ghostly encounters originating from the cemetery, enhanced by rumours of satanic rituals and gravestone robbing. The graveyard dates from 1844, with its last burial having taken place in 1965.

LORD COMBERMERE'S CHAIR
December 1891

Amateur photographer Sybil Corbet took this incredible photograph in the library of Combermere Abbey in Cheshire in December 1891. Despite being totally alone at the time of exposure she was later surprised to see that on the plate, a wispy image of a gentleman with no legs was visible on the high-backed chair on the left-hand side of the picture. This chair was a favourite of Lord Combermere's, who had recently been killed in London after being struck by a horse-drawn carriage and was, at the time of the taking of the picture, being interred at Wrenbury, some four miles from the Abbey.

Lord Combermere's home, Combermere Abbey, was founded by Benedictine monks in the 12th century. Later it was the seat of Sir George Cotton and in 1814, Sir Stapleton Cotton, a descendant of Sir George, first took the title 'Lord Combermere'. The building is now in use as a hotel and tourist attraction.

This startling photograph is remarkable under any circumstances, but it is made even more mysterious when one learns that Lord Combermere's legs had been so badly damaged in his accident that, had he lived, he would never have been able to walk again. Strangely, the ghost in the picture appears to have no legs.

THE GREENWICH GHOSTS
19 June 1966

Peter Underwood, the undisputed king of ghost hunters, describes the renowned 'Greenwhich Ghosts' photograph (see over) as 'the most remarkable and interesting that I have seen in half a century of serious psychical investigation'. It was taken by a visiting tourist from Canada at The Queen's House, Greenwich, between 5.15 and 5.30pm on Sunday 19 June 1966.

The Queen's House in Greenwich was built as a home for the consort of Charles I, Queen Henrietta Maria. It is now part of the National Maritime Museum and retains a fascination in the minds of ghost hunters around the world. The image, which has been analysed by the likes of Kodak and pronounced genuine, was caught by mistake on the Tulip Staircase, an area out of bounds to the public. It was just one of several pictures that Reverend R.W. Hardy had taken, and nothing unusual was seen or witnessed at the time. However, after returning home to British Columbia, Canada, and developing the pictures, one of the strangest ghost photographs of all time came to light – the Greenwich Ghosts photograph.

The realization that they had caught something strange on their film came when the Hardys were showing the pictures to some friends. One of them asked who the figure on the staircase was, to which an astonished and somewhat angry Reverend Hardy said that he had no idea – that there had been no-one around when he had taken the picture. His wife said that she remembered clearly that she had stood patiently waiting for the camera to complete its exposure before relaxing in the knowledge that no-one had walked through the shot. The picture clearly shows a hooded figure climbing the stairs while gripping the banister rail with its left hand, upon which is a large wedding ring. There appears to be a further similar figure just in front of the more pronounced 'ghost', which is also wearing a ring.

Having no previous interest in the paranormal, but now hugely curious, the Reverend and his wife returned to the Queen's House the following month. Along with Brian Tremain they attempted to recreate the effect by using a long exposure and having someone draped in a gown move up the staircase at speed – the result is quite different from the true image.

Speculation has suggested that one of the figures might be that of Queen Henrietta herself, while others accept that they are clearly wearing some sort of monk-like garb and are therefore connected to some religious fraternity. In order to try and discover the identity of the hooded figures The Ghost Club Society were given special permission to conduct a séance within the building, near to the staircase, on Saturday 24 June 1967. Unfortunately this proved fruitless and the identities of the ghostly figures remain unknown. A contemporary account from 2002 does tell of a ghostly apparition witnessed within the building, although this was described as that of a female phantom in quite different apparel to that seen on the picture. The picture of the Greenwich Ghosts has never been fully explained and has stood the test of time and expert analysis for over 40 years.

RIGHT: *Figures photographed on the Tulip Staircase of the Queen's House during normal opening hours of the Museum. The photographer apparently saw nothing.*

OPPOSITE TOP: *The two ghostly figures on the left-hand side of Lady Palmer were not seen at the time the photograph was taken in the Basilica de Le Bois-Chenu, near Domremy, France.*

OPPOSITE BOTTOM: *The ghost of Corroboree Rock appeared in this colour photograph taken in 1959 at an abandoned aboriginal ceremony site in Australia. It has never been explained.*

THE GHOSTS OF THE BASILICA
June 1925

It was during a visit to the Basilica de Le Bois-Chenu, near Domremy in France – to see the installation of a Union Jack commemorating the British dead of the First World War – that an English lady named Miss Towsend accidentally caught an image of two white-clad ghostly figures standing alongside her companion, Lady Palmer. It was June, 1925, and after the flag had been hung, Lady Palmer posed for a photograph taken by her companion. Nothing odd or peculiar was noticed at the time – but later, the two apparitions, which are remarkably clear, showed up on the print.

The Basilica was dedicated to Joan of Arc in 1925 and it has been suggested that the two figures bear a striking resemblance to priests of the time of St Joan. Any possible motives for faking such an image were ruled out and the photograph remains one of the strangest ever taken.

THE CORROBOREE ROCK GHOST
1959

Australia's most famous ghost photograph was taken by Reverend R.S. Blance at Corroboree Rock in 1959. The rock is a natural wonder, which lies in the outback approximately 42 kilometres (26 miles) from Alice Springs. The area is well known as a place of sacred power where aborigines once carried out initiation ceremonies.

The reverend was alone at the time the picture was taken, yet standing amidst the undergrowth is a distinct and semi-transparent figure adorned with a headdress with one arm raised. Perhaps this is the ghost of an aboriginal tribesman bedecked in a ritual gown? Never proved as a fake, this image has been accepted by most as genuine, especially since it was taken by a minister of the church.

ABOVE: *Is this Prestbury's infamous 'Black Abbot' beginning a moonlit manifestation one cold evening in November 1990, or a simple fake created by a double-exposure?*

THE BLACK ABBOT OF PRESTBURY
22 November 1990

The quaint and picturesque village of Prestbury on the outskirts of Cheltenham in Gloucestershire is well known as one of the contenders for 'the most haunted village in Britain' (the others are Bramshott in Hampshire, with 17 alleged ghosts, and Pluckley in Kent with between 12 and 16 depending on which source you consult). Of the gaggle of spooks said to infest this otherwise tranquil hamlet, the infamous Black Abbot is perhaps the most prevalent. The phantom has been observed on many occasions and is well attested to by locals and visitors alike. He has been described as 'of solid appearance, not wispy, transparent or ghostlike in any way', and falls into the category of 'anniversary hauntings', appearing at Christmas and Easter as well as on All Saints Day. One particular sighting of note resulted in a motorcyclist having to swerve violently in the road in order to miss what he later described as 'a figure in black robes, which appeared from nowhere'. On other occasions he has been seen floating around the grounds of The Priory – a large house next to the Church of St Mary. Folklore has linked the Abbot to 'Reform Cottage' on Deep Street as he is often seen drifting silently along the path from the graveyard where he traditionally materializes and begins his spectral wanderings toward the cottage garden – a former burial ground for priests living under rule. It is recorded in a variety of publications that the church itself was exorcised to put an end to the frequent visits of the ghost, but this has not prevented him from lingering among the ivy-clad gravestones, observing the occasional burial from afar or surprising visitors by his sudden disappearance.

This now well-known photograph of the Abbot was taken by Derek Stafford one cold evening in November 1990. Derek is on record as stating that he saw nothing out of the ordinary at the time of the exposure and that the shadowy outline of a robed figure is genuine. It is easy to dismiss this image as that of a simple double-exposure, or perhaps a product of elaborate fakery, and critics have also claimed that it is so perfectly 'staged' that it must be a hoax. However, many years later the picture is still unexplained and remains, to some, irrefutable proof that the Black Abbot of Prestbury is a very real phenomenon indeed.

THE HOODED MAN

3 February 1999

This image of an alleged ghost was taken by a paranormal investigator during an investigation of Ellesmere Port Boat Museum in Merseyside. Interestingly, the image was caught during the daytime and seems to fit in with descriptions of former dock workers who might have been in the vicinity in times past.

Examining the ghost closely, it is possible to see that it appears to be a partial manifestation wearing a distinct hood and cloak. Another possibility which has been suggested is that the ghost is wearing a cloth sack of the kind worn by coal-delivery workers. There is a Victorian-era photograph showing this clothing in the museum display.

Adding to the mystery, the ghost photograph was first made public on the 100th anniversary of the death of an 18-year-old dock worker named Samuel Hill. He was employed by the Shropshire Union Railway and Canal Company and was killed during an accident, which took place on Friday 10 February 1899. Could this image caught a century later show his spirit?

LEFT: *This partial apparition was caught by a paranormal investigator at Ellesmere Port Boat Museum on 3 February 1999, but three people who were present at the time claim to have seen nothing.*

THE FLOWER FESTIVAL GHOST

12 September 1993

This ghostly image was caught by photographer Eddie Coxon during a flower festival that was taking place inside Alton parish church in Alton village, Staffordshire. Several people were inside the church at the time of exposure, yet no-one was standing in front of the camera when the picture was taken.

It is possible to see the three-dimensional quality of the ghost in this particular instance, with a pronounced flesh-coloured head, although no facial features, and a wispy blue body-frame which appears to be floating in mid-air.

LEFT: *This three-dimensional faceless phantom was floating unseen around Alton church, Staffordshire, during a Flower Festival in Autumn 1993.*

AN UNINVITED GUEST
22 January 1985

BELOW: St Mary's Guildhall in Coventry City had an uninvited guest during a gala dinner – it was attended by an unseen spook.

A solitary monk appeared in the corner of a photograph taken at St Mary's Guildhall, Coventry, during a dinner of the Freeman's Guild which took place on 22 January 1985. It was only much later on that Lord Mayor Walter Brandish drew attention to the robed figure, which is clearly visible standing in the left-hand corner of the Hall, apparently keeping a close eye on the proceedings. The monk was not seen by anyone during the dinner and is therefore presumed to be a phantom – the 14th-century Guild Hall is known as a haunted hotspot in the city. Speculation has suggested that this may be a Druid as opposed to a monk, although no evidence for this is forthcoming. It is nevertheless a solid and substantial figure, which if a real ghost, is good evidence of survival after death.

THE MAN IN THE CAPE
4 March 1993

It was during a visit to Tutbury in Staffordshire on 4 March 1993 that amateur photographer Brenda Ray decided to take some photographs of the architecture of the town. She experienced nothing out of the ordinary at the time and was surprised when later she found a caped figure walking down the centre of Duke Street in one of her pictures. Another photograph, taken a couple of seconds later, fails to show the figure.

Dressed in a flowing black cape and wearing some kind of tall hat, the unseen figure would surely have appeared in the consecutive picture as well had he been of living, corporeal nature. This picture sparked the interest of *Fortean Times*, the journal of paranormal phenomena, who published it in their issue number 157 in April 2002.

LEFT: Close-up from photograph taken in Tutbury, Staffordshire on 4 March 1993 by Brenda Ray. She did not notice the figure at the time and he does not appear on the next frame taken seconds later.

LEFT: *A headless phantom hound was caught on camera during a tea party in 1916 by a retired Scotland Yard inspector, and today remains unexplained.*

THE PHANTOM DOG
1916

This photograph showing a partially transparent dog, with the head much fainter than the rest of its body, was taken by retired CID Inspector Arthur Springer, formerly of Scotland Yard. It was taken during a tea party in 1916 and the appearance in the print of a ghostly dog remains unexplained. Due to the photographer's former profession, it is thought unlikely to have been faked, with no obvious motive for deception.

THE TWO-HEADED DOG
1926

In one of the strangest manifestations ever caught on camera, Lady Hehir can be seen accompanying her Irish Wolfhound, Tara. The image was taken by Mrs Filson in September 1926, six weeks after the death of a cairn puppy named Kahal, which had been inseparable from Tara. The head peering around the rear of the wolfhound was recognized as that of the dead puppy – perhaps the spirit of the dog refused to leave its earthly playmate?

LEFT: *The face of a dead puppy stares around its living playmate in a picture dating from 1926. It was not seen at the time the picture was taken, although the location had been a favourite playing spot during its lifetime.*

THE GHOST KITTEN
August 1925

A curious photograph dating back to 1925 was taken in Switzerland by a Major Wilmot Allistone. Although nothing was seen at the time of exposure, as is most often the case, a ghostly kitten appears nestling in the hands of one member of the family in the picture.

What is odd is that this white kitten was recognized by the family, who explained that it had been mauled and killed, presumably by a dog, weeks before the picture was taken, and was certainly not in the hands of the child at the time.

A GRAVE SECRET
1947

Joyce Andrews died aged 17 in 1945, and was buried in a churchyard in Gatton in Queensland, Australia, next to her brother Cecil who had passed away in 1942. Their mother visited the grave one day and decided to take a picture of the headstone. When she had her pictures developed a young female child could be seen staring out of the picture while apparently perching at the side of the grave.

Assumed at first to be a double-exposure, this was later eradicated as a possible explanation as no pictures of children had been taken on the film. A researcher named Tony Healy took up the case and noted that the graves of two infant female children lay close by – it is suggested that this ghost photograph shows one of their spirits.

LEFT: *A ghostly girl looks into the lens of Mrs Andrews's camera during a visit to the grave of her children in Gatton, Queensland, Australia – yet no such child was seen at the time.*

THE PHANTOM MONK OF NEWBY
1963

One of the most noted and reproduced images of an alleged spectre was taken by the Reverend Kenneth Lord – Vicar of Newby in North Yorkshire, in his own parish church. Despite more than 40 years of speculation, it has never been proved a fake, and still generates heated discussion between researchers of the paranormal. It has been examined at length for signs of double-exposure, which has now been ruled out as a possible explanation.

The photograph was taken on a quiet day when the church was deserted. Nothing was seen through the viewfinder at the time, yet when the prints were developed a tall eerie image of a cowled figure draped in black robes and with a strange 'melting' face was seen. It is quite a startling image to see a transparent ghostly figure stare apparently right into the lens of the camera, but who he is, and why he haunts the church is a mystery. The church dates back to 1870 and prior to this photograph was not generally thought to be haunted. However, one local, 72-year-old Louella Sanderson, believes it is. She is on record as saying 'I have often felt the presence of a spirit [i.e., a non-divine 'ghost'] in the chapel during services'. Reverend Lord was taking the picture as a record of the flower arrangements, which had been freshly displayed upon the altar that can be seen behind – and 'through' – the spectre, which stands nine feet tall! In his book *Ghosts and How to See Them*, author Peter Underwood reports that the image was analysed by a Home Office Laboratory, which was unable to explain it, or replicate the same effect, and therefore concluded that it was of unexplainable origin.

OPPOSITE TOP: *Nestled against a toy rabbit held in the hands of a child in August 1925 is a second animal face – that of the family's kitten, which had been killed weeks before the picture was taken.*

BELOW: *This startling image of a nine-foot-tall cowled figure with a melting face was photographed in Yorkshire in the early 1960s – it remains unexplained after years of analysis.*

Chapter 4

The History of Spirit Communication

In this chapter we will look at how, through the ages, people have tried to make contact with the spirit world. In ancient times, rituals and fire dances were thought to open the gate between the land of the living and that of the dead, and it was believed that at certain times of the year, such as Hallowe'en, conversing with spirits was easier because the veil between these two worlds was thinner. However, modern techniques have replaced these archaic forms of spirit communication, and today electronic voice phenomena and modern mediumship are at the forefront of techniques used by paranormal investigators.

We will also explore divination – the technique of divining the future by spiritual means – and discover the origins of well-known spiritual tools including the scrying mirror and the tarot cards. Where did these forms of communication begin and how do they work? Previously thought to be the tools only of shamans, mediums and psychics, an entire industry of the paranormal is now supported by merchandising such items and making them available to the masses. The onslaught of Internet shopping has also spurred on the increase in availability of divination tools, bridging the gap between the USA, where they have been prevalent for some time, and the United Kingdom, where the surge really only began after the turn of the new millennium.

SCRYING

PREVIOUS PAGE: *The crystal ball has long been an archetype of divinatory practice.*

BELOW: *It is thought that by staring into the murky depths of a crystal ball, it is possible to see into the future.*

The word 'scrying' is thought to derive from an ancient English word 'descry', which means 'to reveal', and revelation is what the art of scrying, in whatever form, is all about. The practice of staring into the depths of a reflective surface to try and commune with spirits is ancient, dating back to the origins of Egypt in 3000BC. Hathor, the goddess of love and joy was one of many revered deities, and it was believed that she carried with her a bright shield in which the truth would always be reflected. From a section of her shield she forged the first 'magic mirror' in which the percipient would be able to see the images of those long dead and acquire knowledge from the world of the spirits. In Persia, the Cup of Jamshid was a goblet which, according to legend, was used by practitioners of esoteric sciences to observe the universe. It was filled with an elixir of immortality, which revealed deep truths to those that observed it.

The act of scrying, by staring into the depths of a cloudy crystal or a shiny reflective surface with no point of focus, is thought to put the scryer into a form of trance, which opens up the psychic mind to images from the other side. These images can be used to divine outcomes in the future or to answer questions posed to the spirits 'seen' during the scrying.

Crystallomancy

There are many forms and mediums of scrying, the most popular being the crystal ball, a highly-polished orb of quartz crystal, or sometimes glass, which sits atop a steady holder. It is usually bathed with the smoke of incense to heighten psychic awareness by cleansing the area and focusing the concentration of the scryer. The crystal ball is usually used in a dimly-lit room, perhaps illumined by the flicker of candlelight which will reflect dancing images within the orb. Although people talk of 'seeing' in the crystal ball, they do not mean that they 'see' literally. The crystal ball, or other scrying instrument, is merely a focus for the inner eye or mind's eye of the percipient or medium who is using it, and the images themselves are not a physical reality within the tool. Crude rock crystals might also be used in Crystallomancy if the percipient prefers a more natural tool. Other forms of Crystallomancy – which means divination by use of a reflected surface – include the Dark Mirror: a black mirror which is stared at until imagery is 'seen' in the mind's eye. In witchcraft, this 'dark mirror' is forged under moonlight and has a lid which shuts over the glass during daylight hours – it must never be opened in sunlight lest it lose its magical ability to see into the shadow realms.

Dream Scrying

Dream Scrying was another form of Egyptian spirit communication which is recorded as far back as 2000BC. Those using this form of scrying had to adhere to a strict ritual in order that the spirits would speak to them through their dreams. It was forbidden to speak to any other living soul on the eve of the Dream Scrying. No consumption of food or drink, or engagement in sexual activity was allowed, the body being fasted for the experience to come. After having bathed and anointed your temples with consecrated oil,

LEFT: *The art of reading tea leaves is as popular today as it has been in the past.*

your intention or question had to be written on a fresh strip of linen before being put into a plain oil lamp. The lamp had to be lit and placed beside the bed as the only source of light in the chamber. Having knelt before the lamp, you had to speak the following invocation aloud:

Thoth I invoke, blessed power of dreams divine,
Angel of future fates, swift wings are thine
Great source of oracles to humankind,
When stealing soft, and whispering to the mind,
Through sleep's sweet silence and the gloom of night,
Thy power awake the sight,
To silent souls the will of heaven relates,
And silently reveals their future fates.

The lamp would then be extinguished, and with a clear mind the percipient would drift off to sleep to see the answers to his or her questions in symbolic imagery, or hear direct voices in their dream.

Tasseomancy

The art of reading tea leaves is another form of scrying, known as Tesseography or Tasseomancy. Although widely thought of as the practice of gypsies, its origins actually lie in Asia and the Middle East, where the reading of not only tea leaves but also coffee and wine sediments were also popular.

When the interest in the mystical arts was growing in the Victorian era the practice became a parlour game in which fortunes would be told by observing the shapes and patterns left in the tea cup after the brew had been enjoyed. In some instances a special cup would be used and twisted several times before revealing the pattern of the leaves. Very similar to the shapes often formed in cloud formations, it is sometimes possible to 'see' images in the leaves which act as symbolic markers for the person reading them.

OPPOSITE BOTTOM: *The ancient Egyptians believed that symbolic imagery appearing in dreams often had a hidden meaning.*

PYROMANCY

ABOVE: *In Pyromancy, the flames of the fire flicker with messages of what lies ahead.*

Divination by means of fire is known as Pyromancy – the word comes from the Greek *pyros* meaning fire, and *manteia* meaning divination. It is a popular practice among witches and is probably one of the earliest forms of scrying in the history of the haunted world. In China during the Neolithic period 'oracle bones' – the shoulder blades of oxen – were thrown onto huge fires and the ensuing cracks that appeared in the bones were observed as portents (this was known as Scapulomancy). Pyromancy was also practiced at the Temple of Athena in ancient Athens.

In its basic form Pyromancy is the act of watching the flames of a fire either from a candle, a hearth, a bonfire or other source, and interpreting the shapes of the dancing flames into symbolic images. There are many forms of the art of pyromancy, including: Alomancy, which is divination performed by casting salt onto a fire; Daphnomancy or Empyromancy, which is divination performed by burning laurel leaves; Capnomancy, or the interpretation of smoke tendrils; Botanomancy, which involves burning plants on a scrying fire; Plastromancy, which is divination by lighting fires in turtle plastrons; and Osteomancy, involving the burning of bones as described above.

HYDROMANCY

BELOW: *Hydromancy can be practiced using a bowl of water, or at a stream or river.*

As fire is used in Pyromancy to contact the spirit realms, water is used in Hydromancy for the same purpose. In water divination the tool might be a river, stream, fountain or the sea. Or it could be a containment of water in a special bowl or cauldron. Even the formations of falling rain can be interpreted by those with second sight. It is believed that the patterns suggest images to the subconscious psychic eye.

In Hydromancy, which is currently enjoying a renewed popularity, the reader will watch the movements of water as it flows or watch the ripples as pebbles or other items are thrown into it. The movements spell the answers to questions or problems posed to the spirit land, interpreted by the watcher. In other forms of Hydromancy a still bowl of water might be used in the same way that a dark mirror would be stared into, its depths and no single point of focus pushing the percipient into a form of trance where communication with the other side is made easier.

DOWSING

The practice of dowsing – or locating objects, items or people, by psychic and telluric means – is thought to date back over 7,000 years, although its exact origins are unclear. Certainly images of forked rods, commonly used in the practice, can be seen in Egyptian imagery and were known to have been utilized by ancient Chinese kings. Throughout the Middle Ages it is thought that dowsers were used to ascertain the location of coal deposits in Europe.

Whether there is any objective reality to the power of dowsing is a moot point, with current scientists unable to understand how it works. Those who practice dowsing may label themselves as psychics or paranormal investigators, but just as many will say they have no spiritual or psychic leanings whatsoever. So if two opposing sides are both producing the same results it is clearly not necessary to 'believe' in order to see the effects of dowsing – indeed some large corporations employ dowsers to examine areas where they are thinking of drilling, to discover if this ancient practice can work for them.

The famous dowser Tom Lethbridge wrote a book in 1976 entitled *The Power of the Pendulum* in which he discusses his experiments within the practice. Using a pendulum he discovered that the length of twine or string upon which the pendulum is mounted is of paramount importance to its ability to dowse. Pendulum dowsing is a very popular form of the practice but the more traditional forked rod or dowsing rods are still used in modern society. During the 1930s there was a lot of activity in Europe with the formation of The British Society of Dowsers, and the term 'radiesthesia' was coined by French priest Alex Bouly, based on the Latin words for 'radiation' and 'perception' – although the term 'dowsing' is still used more often.

Descriptions of why and how dowsing works differ from source to source but a common belief points to a kind of earth or 'telluric' energy, which affects the rods, causing them to move. What is unexplained is the link between the intentions of the dowser and the apparent understanding by the rods, pendulum or willow branch, of these intentions.

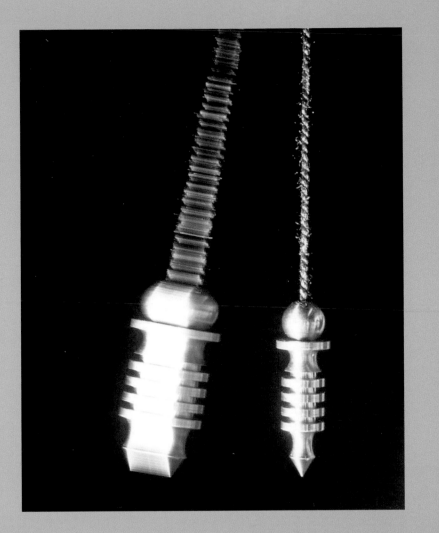

ABOVE: *Some dowsers prefer using a pendulum rather than the traditional forked or dowsing rods. It is thought the length of the twine or string from which the pendelum swings is of paramount importance to the effectiveness of the dowsing.*

Pendulum Dowsing

In pendulum dowsing, the questioner uses a simple weight on a string of cotton or twine to receive answers from the spirit world by the movements of the pendulum. Usually a crystal or ring, the weight will move in either a circular or backwards-and-forwards motion. In most cases circular spinning is accepted as a positive or 'yes' answer, while backwards-and-forwards indicates a 'no' or negative response. It is thus possible to put direct questions to the inhabitants of the spirit world, although whether this really is a way to contact the beyond or simply movements created by the person holding the pendulum is a matter of belief.

In recent years this form of psychic dowsing has become widely popular with those seeking ghosts, with the dowser asking the pendulum to spin at points in a haunted house

where spirit activity is strong. In other uses a pendulum will be placed over a map to ascertain the location of a lost object or person. This method was made popular by the American TV series *Charmed*, where the diviner then 'follows the pull' to the desired place.

Dowsing with Rods

The traditional dowsing rods are two L-shaped metal wands, usually made of brass or copper, although other metals are used, which 'guide' the dowser either by pointing in the direction he or she should walk or by crossing over or parting to indicate a 'yes' or 'no' response. As is the case for the pendulum, the use of dowsing rods to pinpoint 'paranormal energy centres' is now commonplace among researchers in the psychic field. The theory is that the energies created by the presence of spirits can be picked up by the rods. It is also thought that leylines can be identified by asking the rods to cross over when the dowser walks across the invisible line. However the rods work, they do seem to have a high success rate and apparently can be used after a couple of minutes' practise by a novice.

In recent years, dowsing rods have been used as a direct link to the spirit world, where the dowser will stand in a haunted location and ask the ghost to use the rods to answer direct questions posed to him or her by moving the rods across each other for 'yes' or apart for 'no'. Surprisingly, this activity has proved to work in many instances, yet has no scientific basis of evidence to explain why.

ABOVE: *A dowser uses a pair of rods to ascertain the location of unseen energies.*

Willow Witching

In Willow Witching, the oldest form of dowsing, a Y-shaped willow branch is clasped firmly by the two-pointed end of the branch, one point in either hand. The dowser then walks over the area to be dowsed. When used to find hidden underground sources of water, this technique is termed Water Witching. The single-pointed end of the branch is said to bend upwards or downwards when over the correct spot.

In modern times this form of dowsing is sometimes employed to ascertain locations of natural oil sources, with the dowser walking across an area until a positive reaction is discovered. This practice can also be used to find lost objects.

LEFT: *A pendulum is used in an attempt to locate a missing person.*

SPIRIT BOARDS

The history of spirit boards, talking boards or witch boards as they are sometimes called, dates back to 1886 when an article in the *New York Daily Tribune* described a new form of spirit communication using a rectangular board on which the alphabet, the numbers one to nine and the words 'Yes' and 'No' were drawn.

Spiritualism was at its height in America when the spirit board made its first appearance. When the Fox sisters of Hydesville claimed they had contacted the ghost of a dead peddler in 1878, becoming instant celebrities and sparking the beginning of Spiritualism, various contraptions were developed and engineered to aid the connection between the spirit world and the new 'mediums' who acted as the messenger between worlds. Many of these early forms of spirit communication were hard to use or produced indecipherable results. The planchette – allegedly designed by a French medium named M. Planchette, although this is disputed by some – was a crude form of communication where the spirit would 'write' a message via a wooden platform on wheels on which a pencil and the medium's hand were placed. Other instruments, for example the psychograph and dial plate, were large and complicated to use. A simpler, purer form of communication was needed – and thus the spirit board was born.

The designer of the first 'talking board' is unknown, but it is generally accepted that William Fuld was responsible for the fusion of the French and German words for 'yes' – *oui* and *ja* – thus naming the most popular and well-known spirit board, Ouija. However, 36 years before the first patent of a talking board in America, Adolphus Theodore Wagner filed patent for a 'Psychograph, or apparatus for indicating persons' thoughts by the agent of nervous electricity' in England on 23 January 1854. The English patent describes the device in great detail, but omits any mention of the board being used to contact the world of the spirit. Instead it describes how the board was a device which expressed the thoughts of the user in physical terms.

LEFT: *Sitters place their hands lightly on a planchette in the hope that a spirit will speak to them.*

ABOVE: *A medium uses a spirit board to receive direct messages from the spirit world.*

BELOW: *Many believe that spirit boards are the key to unlocking the door between this world and the next.*

William Fuld's 'Ouija' was an instant hit across the USA, and was copied and remarketed by a host of other companies who made their own slightly different versions. William was a good businessman, however, and simply produced a cheaper board than his competitors, on one occasion reprinting a competitor's board on the back of his own, thereby giving the customer two boards for the price of one and ensuring that his remained the most popular.

After running his business for 25 years and making a profit of three million dollars from sales of his talking board, William met an unfortunate end on 24 February 1927. He had been supervising building work on a new factory and had made his way to the top of a three-storey building upon which a flagpole was being erected. After slipping, he fell from the roof and suffered concussion and broken ribs, and later died in hospital when a rib punctured his heart.

Following the death of their father, William's children Catherine and William A. Fuld took over the running of the Ouija company, continuing with mass production of the famous talking board and also adding a new metallic version which included flashing lights. Unfortunately, the market could not sustain the new board, which cost three times more than its predecessor, and after a year of low sales the stock was melted down and the project scrapped.

On 23 February 1966, America's largest board-game manufacturer Parker Brothers announced that the Fuld family had sold them all rights to the Ouija board, after they had allegedly made an offer that the Fulds could not refuse, and Parker Brothers remain sole owners of the patent to this day. Although the design of the board has altered several times, it remains one of the most popular board games sold in toy stores across the United States, the latest incarnation being a smaller version with a glow-in-the-dark board. The tag line reads 'It's only a game... isn't it?'

TABLE TILTING

Table Tilting, which began as a popular parlour game and was frequently used by fraudulent mediums to demonstrate manufactured 'phenomena', has since evolved into a communication technique widely used by paranormal investigators and in Spiritualist circles. Those who believe in the spirit world accept that the table is influenced by the dead, who use the table as a medium to communicate with the living through a variety of tapping, rocking, sliding and levitating movements.

The setting is usually a dimly-lit room where a small lightweight table is placed in the centre of a group of sitters. The sitters will each place their hands lightly upon an edge of the table and wait patiently until some kind of vibration or movement is sensed. The presence of a gifted sensitive does not seem to be necessary in order to achieve the desired effect, but whether the force is coming from the world of spirit or from the hands of those willing it to move is a controversial issue.

In 1972 a group of investigators in Toronto, led by a parapsychologist, decided to carry out an experiment to see if they could create an artificial 'ghost' and then contact it to see if the thought-form had independent intelligence. They named their character 'Philip' and gave him a detailed history. Born Philip Aylesford in 1624, he became a knight and fought in the English Civil War. Later in life he fell in love with a gypsy who was burned as a witch and as a result he committed suicide in 1654 aged just 30. Of course, this was all pure fiction, the creation of the imaginations of the sitters, but what happened next intrigued them all...

BELOW: *A table appears to levitate unaided into the air during a seance.*

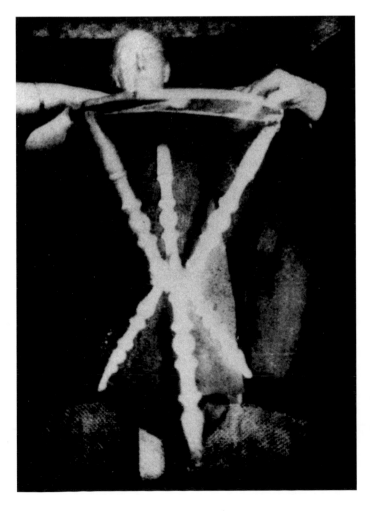

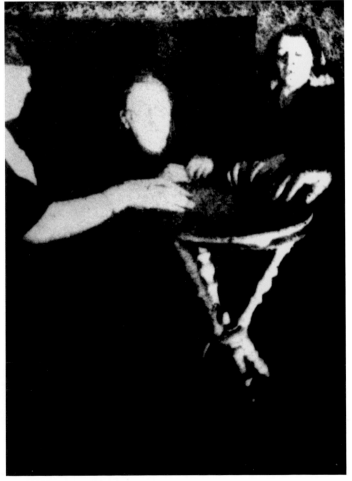

After initial failure for several weeks, the group did appear to receive messages from 'Philip' via a small table around which they sat, trying to communicate with him. Beginning at first with light taps and small phenomena these increased week after week until the table would bounce around in answer to their questions to 'Philip'. On one occasion the table had moved so violently around the room that it had trapped one sitter in the corner, while at other times it would jump towards latecomers, as if welcoming them to the session! Table Tilting phenomena continued for several years and were even recorded on film for all to see, and this spurred other groups around the world to create their own collective-mind monsters, achieving the same results.

So where does this energy come from? Is it from the other side, as the Spiritualists and mediums argue, or is it from the subconscious, as suggested by British psychologist Kenneth J. Batcheldor, who first pioneered the modern-day use of Table Tilting as a parapsychological experiment? Batcheldor believed that the heightened sense of expectation, the atmosphere and the 'belief' in the minds of the sitters was enough to create an energy, and that the medium for this to manifest was the table. He did not believe that the force came from anywhere other than from within the sitters.

Table Tilting continues to be a popular form of communication, enjoying a revival since the dawn of the New Millennium.

RIGHT: *A chair flies across the room while the medium is bound with a cord to eradicate the possibility of foul play.*

ELECTRONIC VOICE PHENOMENA

EVP, or Electronic Voice Phenomena, was first suggested by Thomas Edison who announced in the American magazine *Scientific American* that he had designed and was constructing a machine which would capture the voices of the deceased and record them. His idea had been drawn from the idea that if spirits could be captured on photographs, which was accepted at the time, then surely they could also be caught audibly. Unfortunately he died in 1931, and no records to indicate how such a machine might be manufactured were found among his papers.

The next development in EVP was achieved by Attila von Szalay, who in 1938 managed to record voices on a phonograph record. Von Szalay believed one of the voices to be that of his dead son, and he continued with his research, working with researcher Raymond Bayless in 1956.

In Sweden, a remarkable discovery was made by Friedrich Jurgenson while recording birdsong in his garden in 1959. When he played back the recording the sound of a Norwegian voice discussing the birdsong and giving personal details about Jurgenson was heard. The anomalous 'voice' also gave instructions on how further recordings should be made. Jurgenson followed the instructions, and the result was a record and accompanying book entitled *Voices from the Universe*, released in 1964.

ABOVE: *Electric Voice Phenomena researcher Konstantin Raudive recorded thousands of spirit voices in his laboratory.*

In 1965, Jurgenson met with Latvian psychologist Konstantin Raudive, who was so enthralled by the EVP phenomenon that he devoted himself entirely to its research, resulting in the compilation of over 100,000 recordings being made over several years. Later, Raudive was to become eternally associated with the research he had spent so much time working on, when the term 'Raudive Voices' was coined to describe any type of EVP.

Interest was by now spreading around the world and various organizations sprang up to conduct more research into the technological ghost-hunting phenomenon of EVP. In Germany some time in the 1970s, The Association for Voice Taping Research was formed, while later, in 1982, Sarah Estep founded the American Association – Electronic Voice Phenomena (AAEVP), as a way of helping people learn about, and experience, electronic voice phenomena. The organization has a wide membership and is a not-for-profit organization whose aims are research and teaching. Sarah stepped down in May 2000, handing over the reigns to Tom and Lisa Butler, who are continuing her work in this field.

In 1982, George Meek, an engineer, announced to the world that together with medium William O' Neill, he had built a device named Spiricom which had the ability to contact the spirit world. The concept had been received as a psychic message purportedly from a dead scientist, and later an entity calling itself Doc Nick explained to Meek – through O' Neill – how he should construct the device. In response to the messages Meek founded The Metascience Foundation of North Carolina to make the plans for building Spiricom available to the general public, at no cost. After the initial media flurry there was little success, with critics suggesting that Meek's personal experience had been based on the presence of medium William O' Neill, and not the Spiricom device.

Today EVP research is moving into various other areas of research including haunted houses, communication with extra-terrestrials and people from the future. Other devices such as video, television and computers are now all being used in attempts to record spirit voices, although many believe these 'anomalous' images and sounds are nothing more than partial random broadcasts, which are flitting around us at all times.

Chapter 5
Prominent Figures of the Paranormal

In this chapter we will meet those people who have done the most to shape our knowledge and perception of the haunted world. From ghost hunters of note to parapsychologists, occultists, a witch and even royalty – each have played their role in defining and exploring the unseen world around us. Their legacies have paved the way for modern researchers, psychics and investigators to continue our exploration into realms currently beyond our understanding.

The accomplishments, goals and ideals of each of the people profiled in this chapter would be enough to fill a book alone, and indeed many have written their own autobiography – I recommend that serious students of the paranormal indulge themselves with copies of the same. Within the constraints of this book, my intention is to highlight their key achievements, and identify their areas of influence on our understanding of the haunted world.

ALEISTER CROWLEY

AUTHOR AND OCCULTIST

12 October 1875 – 1 December 1947

PREVIOUS PAGE: Queen Victoria was a passionate supernaturalist.

BELOW: An artist's depiction of 'The Beast 666', otherwise known as Aleister Crowley, the master occultist.

Born Edward Alexander Crowley in Leamington Spa, England in 1875, the notorious and controversial figure of Aleister Crowley is often misunderstood. Despite becoming infamous as 'The Beast 666' – a term he decided to keep after his mother used it to describe him during his early rebellious years – Aleister was an intelligent forward-thinker who achieved much in his 72-year-long life. It is true he spent much of his time going out of his way to obtain notoriety in a number of ways, but what is rather less known is the fact that he was an accomplished mountain-climber, poet and chess master.

Renowned as one of the greatest Occultists of all time, he was personally responsible for the foundation of Thelema – a magical system combining a radical form of philosophical libertarianism with an initiatory system derived from The Hermetic Order of the Golden Dawn, a magical tradition which was itself to influence many 20th-century belief systems including modern Wicca.

Crowley was raised in a Christian family of the Plymouth Brethren whose rigid values were instilled in him from a very early age. His father was a preacher who had amassed a fortune running a lucrative brewery business, and after his death in 1887 the family wealth passed to Edward (known as 'Alick' at the time), who subsequently began dabbling in satanic ritual. He wrote around this time, 'The forces of good were those which had constantly oppressed me. I saw them daily destroying the happiness of my fellow men. Since, therefore, it was my business to explore the spiritual world, my first step must be to get into personal communication with the devil.' Some suggest this was a way of coping with his grief over the loss of his father, and also as an obvious act of rebellion against Christianity.

However, he soon lost interest in the devil after enrolling as a student at Trinity College, Cambridge, reading Poetry and Moral Sciences. Here, he became heavily influenced by Arthur Waite's *The Book of Black Magic and Pacts*. His interest in the occult world was now growing and he left Cambridge in 1898 to join the Hermetic Order of The Golden Dawn in November that year.

As part of the initiation into the Order he studied mysticism with the likes of William Yeats and Arthur Waite, making enemies of both after a short time. He was then introduced to the ideas of Buddhism by Samuel Macgregor Mathers, his mentor at the time – but who also became his enemy and later sued Crowley over a copyright infringement of a public ritual performed by Crowley but, according to Mathers, written by him. Crowley responded by naming the villain in his book *Moonchild* as SRMD – an abbreviated form of Mathers' occult name. By 1900, his relationship with Mathers had broken down and Crowley travelled widely in the East, learning the disciplines of Yoga and Oriental Mysticism. He later travelled to Mexico where he discovered the word 'Abrahadabra' (commonly used in magical scriptures as 'Abracadabra'), using Cabbalistic methods. This word later became part of *The Book of The Law* – a scripture transcribed by Crowley which he allegedly received from an ancient Egyptian god, Horus.

On 12 August 1903, Aleister married Rose Kelly and they honeymooned in Egypt, returning to Cairo in 1904. Rose became tormented during the honeymoon by what she described as attempts by the god Horus to contact Crowley. As a test, Crowley took her to the Boulak Museum in Cairo and asked her to point out the god she spoke of – she identified a wooden funerary stele from the 26th dynasty, The Stele of Revealing, depicting Horus receiving a sacrifice from a priest named Ankh-f-n-Khonsu. Crowley was convinced that Horus was trying to reach him through Rose. He discovered that the museum inventory number allocated to the monument was 666 – a number with which, incidentally, he had identified since childhood – which seemed to reinforce his suspicion.

Crowley subsequently invoked Horus in a private ritual and felt the presence of a shadowy entity calling itself 'Aiwaz'. The messenger informed Crowley that a 'New Magical Aeon' had begun and that he had been chosen as its prophet on earth, and proceeded to recite *The Book of the Law* (also known as *Liber Al vel Legis*, or *Liber Al* for short) to Aleister, which he transcribed and subsequently published. This text, much of it in numerical ciphers, remains in print throughout the world and forms the basis of Thelema – a magical belief system still in use today. Thelemites are members of the OTO – Ordo Templis Orientis – and will commonly pass the salutation and the felicitation 'Love is the Law' to which their addressee will answer 'Love under Will'. It is written in correspondence as 93/93, as these numbers are the gematrical form of the phrases. (Gematria is an ancient Hebrew numerical system, which gave a number to every Hebrew letter and ascribed a certain significance to each number, and therefore to words and sentences.)

Notorious during his own lifetime, Aleister was frequently attacked by the press. In April and May 1923 he was sensationally dubbed 'The Wickedest Man in the World' in *John Bull* – a pictorial publication of the time. It is a tag line which remained with him for the rest of his life.

After being expelled from Italy in 1923 for forming a commune which he named 'The Temple of Thelema' at Cefalu in Sicily, where it is alleged all manner of ritualistic sexual practices were undertaken by himself and his followers, he returned to England.

In 1934, Crowley lost a court case in which he had sued author Nina Hamnett for calling him a 'black magician' in her book *Laughing Torso*, and as a result he was declared bankrupt. He was struggling to overcome a heroin addiction and spent the last years of his life in a boarding house in Hastings, Sussex. During his last years he corresponded with many influential occultists throughout the world including Gerald Gardner (see pages 129–30), who was responsible for the modern resurgence of witchcraft in the UK and founder of 'Gardnerian' Wicca. Crowley is said to have contributed to Gerald's *Book of Shadows* but it is believed his writings were edited by Gerald's High Priestess Doreen Valiente (see pages 129–30), as she found his work offensive.

Also addicted to opium, which had been prescribed to treat his asthma and bronchitis, Aleister Crowley died penniless on 1 December 1947. He was, according to many, one of the greatest occultists the world has ever seen and his legacy lives on through his numerous books and poems, and the Thelamites who still preach his ideals around the world today.

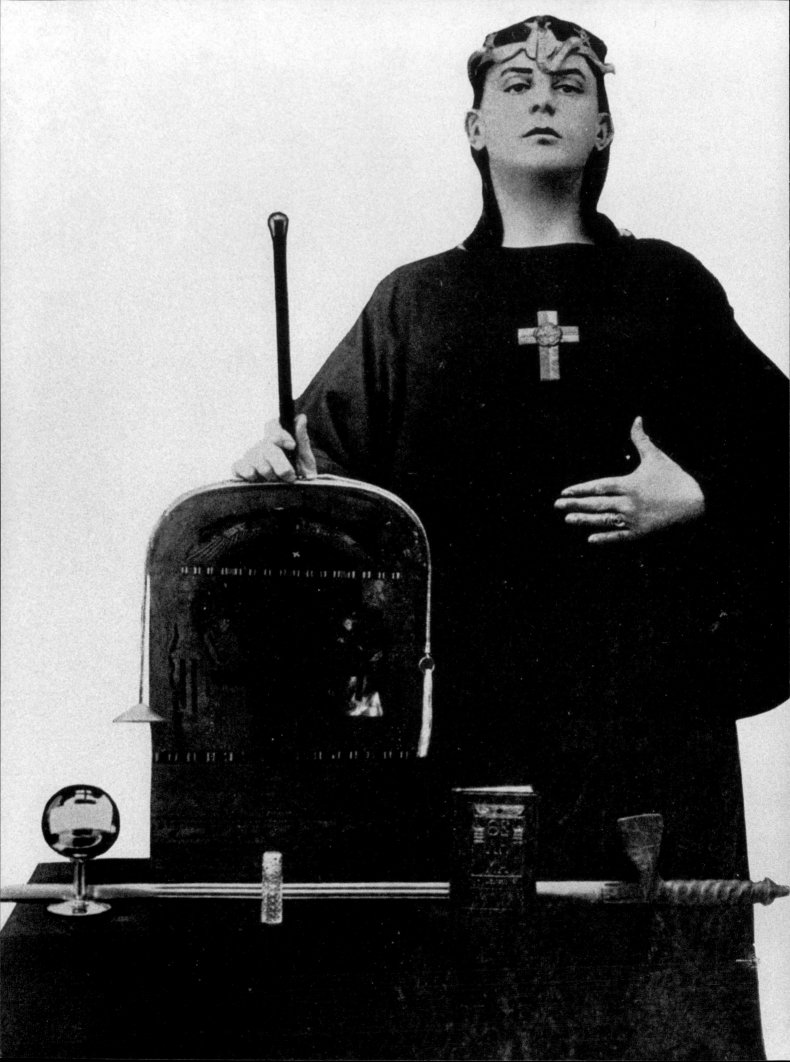

JOHN DEE

SORCERER

13 July 1527–26 March 1608

Born in 1527 at Mortlake (then) on the outskirts of London, John Dee was a mysterious man. After entering St John's College, Cambridge, at the age of 15, and later becoming a Fellow, he graduated as a Bachelor of Arts from Trinity College. After leaving Cambridge, his sense of adventure took him to Belgium where he met Gerardus Mercator, a map-maker from whom he acquired some astronomical instruments and a globe of the world.

Today we associate John Dee with magic and mystery, and his first taste for the subject began while he was working as a mathematics teacher in Paris. There he met the celebrated magician Cornelius Agrippa, and together they explored the hidden worlds that connect us with the realm of spirits. Having returned to England, Dee had already acquired a reputation as an astrologer when he was called to the court of Queen Mary to plot her own horoscope, and thus his first bond with royalty was formed.

After being accused of plotting to murder the Queen, and subsequently being jailed until 1555, even though scant evidence was presented by his accusers, he formed a close friendship with the new queen, Elizabeth, who had been crowned in 1558. Elizabeth introduced Dee to Sir Francis Walsingham, who was in charge of the Secret Service. Following this meeting, Walsingham enlisted Dee to undertake secret business for the Crown, which resulted in whispers suggesting he was using magic to disguise his exploits.

After his first wife died in 1575, following only 12 months of marriage, Dee married again, this time to Jane Fromond, one of the Queen's ladies-in-waiting. His close association with the Queen meant that he was consulted on magical and astrological matters as a matter of course and he used a 'magic mirror' and 'seeing stone' in order to focus his thoughts. In his diary he made detailed records about his own vivid dreams, and those of the Queen, which he believed held valuable symbolism which could be deciphered. To aid him in his quest to contact spirits, something he could not personally achieve, he enlisted Edward Kelley, a former alchemist. Kelley had a colourful past and is alleged to have used necromancy in a churchyard in Lancashire to bring a dead corpse – which he had dug up with an accomplice – back to life. Dee insisted that Kelley only use his gifts to communicate with angels and good spirits and to leave devils and banshees well alone.

OPPOSITE: *An early photograph of Aleister Crowley shows a young passion for the magickal arts.*

BELOW: *Sorcerer and alchemist John Dee travelled widely in search of the strange and fantastic.*

Together Dee and Kelley created a magical system, today known as Enochian Magic. The basis of the system was received from the spirit world by Kelley while staring into a shining crystal. Dee recorded Kelley's observations and proceeded to produce charts and graphs displaying magical symbols and incantations suggested by the spirits. One prolific entity, 'Madimi', was particularly instrumental in the creation of the Enochian system. Dee named one of his daughters after her.

It was a fortunate meeting with Count Adalbert Laski of Poland, in 1583, that was the springboard for Dee and Kelley's next adventure. They had been asked by the Queen to entertain the Count during a visit, and he was so interested in their talk of spiritual beings and experimental investigations of the unknown that he asked them to return to Poland with him. Talk of alchemy – the process of turning base metal into gold – was widespread in this period, and with a possible breakthrough expected, the pair were invited to be the guests of many rich dignitaries, enjoying a celebrity status. However, in 1586 they were accused of sorcery and expelled from Prague.

They were next accepted at the home of Count Wilhelm Rosenberg at Trebon, where their exuberant exploits continued in earnest. It was during this time that Madimi advised Kelley that the pair must share all worldly things – including their wives. This was the beginning of the end of their friendship, for shortly after signing a declaration that they would carry out the spirit's request, the two families parted ways.

After returning to England, Dee was given the wardenship of Christ's College, Manchester, in 1592 by Queen Elizabeth – still his ardent supporter. He returned to his place of birth in 1605, and died aged 81 in 1608.

THE FOX SISTERS

FOUNDERS OF SPIRITUALISM

Katie (1838–92), Leah (1814–90), Margaret (1836–93)

The Fox sisters led tragic lives. Theirs is an unfortunate tale of small-town girls that make good, then are brought down by the very thing that made them. In this case it was not only their alleged ability to communicate with the dead, but also their celebrity status.

There were three sisters: Katie, Margaret and their much older sister, Leah (who was married). At the time that they first experienced mysterious events, Katie was 12 and Margaret was 15. Leah was a good 20 or so years older than her two younger sisters. One evening, in early 1848, the Foxes were made aware of bizarre noises and strange rappings in their house. These noises, it would transpire, were in fact the efforts of a spirit attempting communication. It was allegedly the soul of a man murdered in the house many years before. Soon the Fox sisters were in regular contact with the deceased, and news spread.

Very soon hundreds of people were coming to the small house to bear witness to the psychical phenomena. Many were convinced by the conversations between the spirit and the younger sisters. The sisters' questions were answered by a peculiar loud rap or crack, and in no time at all, the news had become a world-wide sensation. At last, the living could communicate with the dead! And in a way that had no religious connotations and did not seem to involve questions of 'faith'.

The Fox sisters were under suspicion of fraud from some skeptical minds from relatively early on in their celebrity, however. People such as John W. Hurn and Dr Charles Lee stated that the girls were doing nothing more than snapping their knee-joints and the joints in their toes in order to convince people they were in communion with the dead. Even more damning, in 1851 a family relative claimed that Katie had actually confided in her and told her that the strange noises were indeed the snapping of joints, most notably the big toe. In the darkness

KATIE   LEAH   MARGARET

MR ⚭ MRS JOHN D. FOX

THE FOX SISTERS & THEIR PARENTS OF HYDESVILLE, NEW YORK.

LEFT: *The Fox sisters – Katie, Leah and Margaret – founders of the Spiritualist movement, together with their parents.*

of the séance room, nobody would notice the sisters articulating their joints in order to produce the loud noises.

Managed by their older sister, Leah, the Fox sisters became a phenomenon in their own right. It was only after Leah had remarried (following her first husband's death) to a wealthy New York businessman that she ceased to manage her sisters. Katie and Margaret were soon to fall upon hard times. Katie married, but slipped into alcoholism. Margaret, wracked by guilt over the lies about Spiritualism that she and her sister had perpetrated, confessed all to the *New York World*.

I have seen so much miserable deception! Every morning of my life I have it before me. When I wake up I brood over it. That is why I am willing to state that Spiritualism is a fraud of the worst deception... I want to see the day when it is entirely done away with. After my sister Katie and I expose it I hope Spiritualism will be given a death blow.

The confession, however, did no good. Even after the sisters had publicly confessed to the events being a sham, the Spiritualism movement grew and gained more strength. And even though Katie still often held private séances, both sisters toured the country attempting to lecture people on the fraudulent mediums that they had created through their stories. Eclipsed by their own brief celebrity, the sisters went unheeded. Katie died in 1892, spending her last few years as a beggar and a drunk, and Margaret died only a few months after her sister. Both unfortunate sisters were buried in paupers' graves.

ABOVE: The Fox sisters became celebrities, but two of them met with unfortunate ends.

BELOW: The house in Hydesville, New York, where the first signs of supernatural phenomena were alleged to have occurred.

HARRY HOUDINI

CONJURER
6 April 1874–31 October 1926

Harry Houdini was born Erich Weiss in Budapest, in what is now Hungary, on 6 April 1874. His father, Rabbi Mayer Samuel Weiss, and his mother, Cecilia Steiner, moved to the USA in 1878. For some reason, Houdini attempted to hide the exact details of his origin by claiming that he was, in fact, born in Appleton, Wisconsin. The fact of his being born in what is now Hungary was only discovered long after his death.

The Weiss family did, indeed, live in Appleton, where Harry's father was rabbi of the Zion Reform Jewish Congregation. Shortly after this, the Weiss family moved to New York after Harry's father became a United States citizen. It was here that Harry took an apprentice job to a locksmith. It is widely believed that it was here that Harry first learned the masterful art of opening locks without the aid of a key!

Having had a life-long interest in all things magical, in 1891, Harry (still called Erich at this point) became a professional magician. He called himself Harry Houdini, as a tribute to one of his greatest influences, the French conjuror Jean Eugene Robert Houdin. By adding the 'i' Harry became Houdini – or, in French, 'like Houdin'. His early career was dominated by traditional card acts, but Harry was also fascinated by escape acts. Taking this to vaudeville, Harry soon became a sensation. In 1900, Harry toured Europe and returned a celebrity. Some people – Sir Arthur Conan Doyle for one – credited Harry with supernatural forces. This enraged Harry. He knew, better than anybody, that it was all illusion and simple trickery. 'Simple' for Harry, that is – he had been known to dislocate his shoulders in order to escape straitjackets, as well as regurgitate small keys!

It was after the death of his mother, sometime in the 1920s, that Harry Houdini concentrated his efforts on exposing mediums and psychics. In order to do this, Harry would often examine their claims of supernatural powers, not from a scientific stance, but instead from a magical and conjuring point of view. The tricks that could fool science could not fool Harry, and he began a blitz on those that claimed contact with the dead but were in fact deceiving unfortunate people, sometimes for money, although more often than not for celebrity status.

As a member of the *Scientific American* editorial committee, Houdini offered a huge cash prize to any so-called psychic who could prove to him, beyond any reasonable shadow of a doubt, that they truly had supernatural powers and could contact the dead. Needless to say, the cash prize was never won. And the money is still on the table today, thanks to the likes of James Randi, conjurer and author, who has offered an enormous cash prize to any medium who is willing to take up his challenge (most notably American psychic and author Sylvia Brown).

To prove a final point, shortly before his death of peritonitis in 1962, Harry Houdini concocted a secret code. If it were at all possible to communicate with the dead, Houdini would appear at a séance and inform his wife, Bess, of the key to the secret code via the séance's medium. Amazingly, the code was cracked by a medium called Arthur Ford. Unfortunately, later in life, Bess admitted that she had in fact given Arthur Ford the code beforehand in order to announce a successful communication between the living and the dead. Houdini's greatest escape act had come to nothing.

BELOW: *It was thought that Harry Houdini had communicated with his wife following his death in 1962, but this was later found to have been a hoax perpetrated by his wife together with a medium called Arthur Ford.*

NOSTRADAMUS

PROPHET

14 December 1503–2 July 1566

The world's most famous occult prophet is Nostradamus – real name Michel de Nostredame. His famous book of world prophecies was first published in 1555 and it has remained in print in one form or another ever since. He was born in Saint Rémy de Provence in December 1503, one of eight children of parents Jaume and Reynière. Due to the popular interest in his prophecies, his place of birth has become a tourist attraction drawing great crowds every year.

As a student he studied at the University of Avignon for his baccalaureate, but was forced to leave after only a year when the building was closed due to an outbreak of the plague. He became an apothecary and undertook a doctorate in medicine at the University of Montpellier, but was later expelled when his tutors discovered that he had been working as an apothecary – a profession of which they did not approve. After leaving, he continued his work with herbs and he is credited with having created a special 'rose pill', which allegedly warded off the plague.

He married in 1531, after travelling to Agen, but sadly lost his wife and two children to the plague in 1534. Following this tragedy he travelled widely through France and Italy before returning to France in 1545 and working to stop a plague outbreak in Marseille. In 1547, he settled in Salon de Provence, marrying a wealthy woman named Anne Ponsarde. Together they raised three sons and three daughters in a house which still stands today.

It was around 1550 when he began moving away from medicine and towards a more occult way of life. Travelling through Italy he noticed that – no doubt as a consequence of the broadening intellectual horizons engendered by the Renaissance – people seemed to be becoming much more open minded. He capitalized by writing an Almanac, naming himself as 'Nostradamus' for the first time on its cover.

The book was an instant success and he subsequently wrote one every year. Combined, they contain over 6,000 prophecies as well as calendars and moon charts. As a result of the wide distribution of his Almanacs, prominent members of the nobility asked Nostradamus for advice and horoscopes. He was becoming a celebrity.

His next, and most well known, work was a book of one thousand quatrains first published in 1555. The tome is a collection of undated prophecies – which Nostradamus claimed to have received through dreams and visions – for the future of the world, written in an arcane manner which is not easy to understand, including entries in Latin, Greek and Italian. When published as The Prophecies, the book received a mixed reaction with opposing views dubbing him either a 'servant of evil' or a 'spiritually inspired prophet'.

TOP: *Michel de Nostredame, whose prophecies remain in print centuries after his death.*

BOTTOM: *A copy of Nostradamus's famous book,* The Prophecies.

ABOVE: *A statue of Nostradamus stands in Saint-Rémy de Provence, his place of birth.*

One admirer was Catherine de Medici, Queen Consort of King Henry II of France. She called Nostradamus to Paris to discuss his visions and as a result he was made Counsellor and Physician in Ordinary to the King.

Nostradamus died a wealthy man, bequeathing his fortune to his second wife. He is said to have predicted his own death, telling his secretary on the evening of 1 July 1566; 'You will not find me alive by sunrise'. In the morning he was found dead. Buried in a local chapel, his remains were later moved to the Collegiale St Laurent, in Salon, where they remain today.

ELLIOTT O' DONNELL

GHOST HUNTER, AUTHOR AND ACTOR
1872–1965

Elliott O'Donnell was born into a family that claimed descent from the famous Irish Chieftain 'Red Hugh', who fought against the English during the 16th century. One of Ireland's oldest and most honoured families, it was said to have a 'Banshee' – a spirit of portent, which wails at the time of death of a family member.

Elliott was an accomplished ghost hunter and writer, authoring more than 50 collections of supernatural tales which he had collected and witnessed throughout his life. He maintained that his tales were true, although sceptics have suggested that his artistic flair might have seeped into his 'true' accounts. He also wrote several works of fiction, the first being *For Satan's Sake*, which was published in 1905.

He was educated at Clifton College in Bristol, and later in Dublin. When he left Dublin he enjoyed a spell working in America on a ranch, returning to England to train as an actor in 1894. After serving in the army as an entertainer, he took to the stage. During a long career in which he played many roles on TV and in film, Elliott continued writing and developing his passion for all things ghostly. His initial interest had been sparked by an encounter in his college days, when an unseen spirit which had tried to strangle him – a tale he often related on television and in magazine articles on both sides of the Atlantic. The night began with the usual pre-bedtime routine in his shared college digs on Waterloo Road in Dublin, but as Elliott lay waiting for sleep to take him a sound brought his attention to the other side of the room where a black amorphous shape was rising from the floor. Within moments it had leapt across the chamber and lunged down upon him, the sensation of skeletal fingers jabbing at his throat. Consumed with fear, pain and disbelief, he fought with the 'being' before passing out through lack of oxygen. When he came round the phantom assailant was nowhere to be found, and his quest to find out what exactly had happened to him had just begun. This was not, however, his first sighting of a ghost – as a young child he had memories of watching an elemental spirit which was covered in spots.

In later life, as a celebrated ghost hunter, his books captured large audiences – his colourful writing style ensured that even the most mundane tale would be related in a dramatic fashion. His books cover a large geographic area, reflecting a love for travel and sense of adventure. He died aged 93, leaving a legacy of literature, much of which is still in print today.

BELOW: *Elliot O'Donnell travelled throughout the country in search of ghoulish ghosts and spirit animals.*

HARRY PRICE

PSYCHIC RESEARCHER AND AUTHOR

17 January 1881–29 March 1948

Harry Price is considered to be one of the most colourful psychic researchers to have worked in the field. It is often alleged that his research was more theatrical than empirical, but his name is synonymous with one legendary haunting: Borley Rectory (see pages 30–5). Price's interest in the paranormal began at an early age. Founder of the Carlton Dramatic Society, he wrote a small drama concerning poltergeist activity, based – as was always the case with Harry – on real events that had happened to him when staying in a haunted house somewhere in Shropshire.

Later, the young Harry Price would claim in a press release that he had been able to conduct space-telegraphy, capturing the image of a spark upon a photographic plate between a transmitter and a receiver positioned between the summit of a hill and a church between Hatchem and Brockley. Also, that he had happened upon rare antiquities while excavating in Greenwich Park. There, Price alleged, he discovered a silver ingot from the time of Emperor Honorius (384–423 AD). Further investigations into both these claims resulted in accusations that both the silver ingot and the event of space-telegraphy were falsifications.

BELOW: *The great ghost hunter Harry Price inspects an arcane text of magickal literature.*

LEFT: *Harry in his laboratory, where he developed sophisticated equipment to test psychic phenomena.*

Such counter-claims did not stop Price, however, and in 1922 he struck gold by exposing spirit photographer William Hope to be a fake. He then began to work closely with mediums and experiment upon claims of their powers, founding the Laboratory of Psychical Research. Harry was also appointed foreign research officer to the American Society of Psychical Research.

In 1929, Price began his decade-long investigation into the haunting of Borley Rectory, in Essex. Home of the Reverend Henry Bull, the rectory was apparently plagued by a host of supernatural phenomena including a phantom nun, a ghostly apparition of a black coach and horses, as well as eerie sounds and whispers echoing through the long passageways and locked rooms of the rectory. Following these disturbances, spirit writing had begun to mysteriously appear upon the walls. The Rev. Henry Bull stayed on at Borley Rectory for six years before finally moving out, and at that time, Price moved in. Price and his fellow researchers stayed at the rectory between 1937 and 1939. As their experiments began, supernatural activity increased to alarming levels. Price recorded the events in his bestselling books *The Most Haunted House in England* and *The End of Borley Rectory*.

Borley Rectory burned down in 1939, and the Society of Psychical Research carried out an independent investigation on Price in 1956. The Society concluded that Price had exploited the reputation of the rectory, embellished events for a good story – that he was, in effect a fraudster. Considering that Price died in 1948, eight years before the Society's investigation, he hardly had a chance to defend himself against these accusations.

After Borley Rectory, Price continued his research into such baffling cases as the medium Helen Duncan, whom Price later exposed as a fake. Instead of producing ectoplasm, as she claimed, Helen Duncan had swallowed cheesecloth and vomited it out at the sitting, to the amazement of her sitters.

Outside of his psychic research, Price was involved in the creation of the illustrious National Film Library (today known as the BFI, or British Film Institute), and was even a founding member of the Shakespeare Film Society.

Harry Price died in March 1948. His reputation as a showman and psychical trickster is a strange contradiction to that of the Harry Price who exposed fraudulent mediums. We will never know the truth for, as far as we know, Harry Price has not *yet* proffered up an explanation for the controversies from beyond the grave!

WILLIAM ROLL

PARAPSYCHOLOGIST
3 July 1926–Present day

ABOVE: *Parapsychologist William Roll has investigated paranormal occurences throughout both the UK and the USA.*

Born in the province of Bremen in Germany on 3 July 1926, William Roll is one of the most distinguished researchers into the field of psychical phenomena. William's father was American Vice-Consul, so upon his return to the States William enrolled at university, attending the University of California in 1947, achieving his Bachelor of Arts in 1949, majoring in both philosophy and psychology. After a year of graduate work in sociology, William then went to Oxford University to do research in parapsychology under Professor H.H. Rice, which he did until 1957. He recieved an M.Litt. degree for his thesis, entitled 'Theory and Experiment in Psychical Research,' and became president of the Oxford University Society for Psychical Research. Later that year, Roll joined the staff of the Parapsychology Laboratory at Duke University, in Durham NC, USA. Here he worked closely with Dr J.B. Rhine until 1964, by which time he had made his first investigative research into a haunting and recurrent spontaneous psychokinesis (RSPK). Shortly after this he was elected as the director of the PRF (or Psychical Research Foundation) and was also soon elected as the president of another prominent group, the Parapsychological Association. In 1964, Dr J.B. Rhine retired from the Parapsychology Laboratory and William Roll was subsequently appointed as Professor of Psychical Research and Psychology at West Georgia College in Carrollton, Georgia, USA.

In 1984, William was involved in the Columbus poltergeist case, in which a teenage girl by the name of Tina Resch claimed to be experiencing supernatural poltergeist activity in her family home. All manner of objects were hurled through the air and the family was constantly terrified by the events. The media circus was also an intrusive presence in their home, but as the story unfolded it was soon discovered that Tina was in fact the cause of the 'poltergeist' activity. In staging the events, she was attempting to use the media in order to find her true mother and father (she was adopted). It was only quite by chance that her plan was discovered after a television cameraman accidentally left his camera rolling and managed to capture Tina throwing an object herself.

So, if she really was a hoaxer, then Tina Resch had even managed to convince William Roll of the occurrences. In his book *The Supernatural A-Z*, James Randi states that 'Descriptions given by William Roll … turned out to be of quite impossible sequences'. The video footage along with media hype had managed to create a sensational story that, perhaps, was too good to be true. Had Tina faked the *entire* thing, or had she exploited and imitated genuine poltergeist events in order to fuel media attention to the case? Either way, her desperate story has a tragic footnote – in 1994 she was jailed for the murder of her three-year-old daughter.

William Roll has continued to investigate the paranormal, writing over 100 scientific papers as well as four books, including *The Poltergeist* (1972). He has received a PhD from Lund University in Sweden, and has been a freelance lecturer on parapsychology since the early 1990s. In 2002, he received the Dinsdale Memorial Award – given by the Society for Scientific Investigation – for his study into the RSPK phenomenon.

TROY TAYLOR

PROLIFIC GHOST HUNTER
24 September 1966–Present day

Troy Taylor is the author of more than 40 books about history, hauntings and the unexplained in America, including *Haunted Illinois*, *The Ghost Hunter's Guidebook*, *Weird Illinois* and many others. He is the founder and president of the American Ghost Society, a national network of ghost hunters that collects stories of ghost sightings and haunted houses and uses investigative techniques to track down evidence of the supernatural.

Taylor was born in Decatur, Illinois – a Midwestern city that is steeped in legend and lore. Even the hospital in which he was born is allegedly haunted by a phantom nun. He grew up fascinated with 'things that go bump in the night', as well as the writings of haunted travel writer Richard Winer and legendary ghost hunter Harry Price (see pages 122–3). In school, Taylor was well known for his interest in the paranormal and often took friends on informal ghost tours of haunted places all over downstate Illinois. He would later turn this interest into his full-time career.

In 1989, Taylor started working in a bookstore and a few years later, he wrote his first book on ghosts. It was called *Haunted Decatur* and delved into the ghosts and hauntings of the city where he grew up. He also created a tour that took guests to places that he had written about in the book. The book became an immediate success and its popularity, along with his previous experiences with ghost hunting, established Taylor as an authority on the supernatural. The book and tour led to media and public appearances and numerous requests to investigate ghostly phenomena.

In 1996, Taylor organized a group of ghost enthusiasts into an investigation team and the American Ghost Society was launched, gaining more than 600 members in its first ten years. The organization continues today as one of America's largest and most honoured research groups.

Taylor describes himself as an 'open-minded sceptic' and, while he believes in ghosts, has never found any conclusive proof of their existence outside of his own experiences. His no-nonsense approach to ghosts has appealed to a wide audience and many consider his *Ghost Hunter's Guidebook* a standard manual for ghost research fieldwork. When investigating strange phenomena, Taylor starts with the premise that the cause of the activity is not a ghost, and looks first for all possible natural explanations.

BELOW: *Troy Taylor, one of America's most prolific ghost researchers and founder of the American Ghost Society.*

ABOVE: Author Troy Taylor at an abandoned mausoleum in Illinois, which is purported to have been haunted for many years. In this photograph, Troy points out the damage done to the mausoleum by vandals.

In 1998, Taylor moved his operations, which now included the American Ghost Society, a history and hauntings bookstore and a publishing company called Whitechapel Press, to Alton, Illinois, near St Louis. In Alton, Taylor started his second tour company, Alton Hauntings, which also took guests to local haunted places in the small Mississippi River town. He would go on to put the place on the map as 'one of the most haunted small towns in America'.

Taylor remained in Alton until 2005, when he returned to Decatur. By then he had also established two more tour companies, one in Springfield, Illinois, and another company that arranges overnight stays in haunted places. He also took over the management of a tour company in Chicago. All of the tours, including those in Decatur and Alton, are organized under the name of the Illinois Hauntings Ghost Tours. Taylor also continues the operation of Whitechapel Press, which specializes in ghost-related titles and has published more than a dozen authors.

Along with writing about the unusual and hosting tours, Taylor is also a public speaker on the subject of ghosts and hauntings, and has spoken to literally hundreds of private and public groups on a variety of paranormal subjects. In the USA he has appeared in newspaper and magazine articles about ghosts and has been interviewed hundreds of times for radio and television broadcasts about the supernatural. He has appeared in a number of documentary films, several television series and in one feature film about the paranormal. He currently resides in Central Illinois with his wife, Haven, in a decidedly unhaunted house.

PETER UNDERWOOD FRSA

GHOST HUNTER AND PRESIDENT OF THE GHOST CLUB SOCIETY

16 May 1923–Present day

Peter Underwood, the UK's undisputed king of ghost hunters, was born at Letchworth Garden City in May 1923. He has spent almost 60 years exploring the supernatural world around us and is known throughout the world for his lectures, broadcasts and numerous books. He took part in the very first 'official' investigation of a haunted house, and has attended physical and mental séances at the invitation of The College of Psychic Studies.

In 1947, Peter joined The Society for Psychical Research and The Ghost Club at the invitation of the late Harry Price. The Ghost Club ceased to function shortly after Price's sudden death in 1948, and Peter helped to resuscitate the club in 1951. In 1993, he was elected President and Life President of The Ghost Club Society, a leading UK-based serious study group of which the author is a member.

Peter has contributed articles on psychical research, Spiritualism, poltergeists and Harry Price to the 12-volume *Everyman's Encyclopaedia*, 1958 and 1967 editions. Peter's first book to be published was *A Gazetteer Of British Ghosts*, subsequently published as a *Gazetteer Of British, Scottish and Irish Ghosts* by Bell Publishers of New York, and as *The A-Z Of British Ghosts* in 1992. This publication was the first comprehensive volume of alleged ghosts and haunted houses in the British Isles. In the years that followed he wrote more than 40 books, including two biographies, an autobiography and a *Dictionary of the Supernatural*, but mainly books on ghostly activity, dowsing, vampirism, exorcism and reincarnation. He co-wrote *Ghosts Of Borley – Annals of the Haunted Rectory* with Dr Paul Tabori, whom he succeeded as Literary Executor to The Harry Price Estate.

He played a leading role in the TV documentary *The Ghost Hunters,* which was screened for six years in succession on the BBC from 1996. He has appeared in more than 30 television programmes and more than 100 radio broadcasts including *Start The Week*, *Midweek*, *Late Nite Line Up*, *Panorama* and *The Jimmy Young Show*. He also wrote and narrated the Radio series *The Ghost Trail* and was the subject of a radio profile which was selected for *Pick Of The Week*.

BELOW: *Peter Underwood, FRSA, the undisputed 'King of the Ghost Hunters' and president of the UK-based Ghost Club Society.*

RIGHT: *Few ghost hunters can claim as prolific a career as Peter Underwood. He has been investigating hauntings for over 50 years.*

Throughout his life Peter has lectured nationally, including giving invited appearances at the universities of Oxford, Cambridge, Sheffield, Birmingham and Sussex. He has also delivered lectures to The Society for Psychical Research, The Unitarian Society for Psychical Studies, and The Savage Club.

A serving member of many societies, including The Savage Club and The Society of Authors, he is also Vice President of The Unitarian Society for Psychical Studies, and in 1987 was elected a Fellow of the Royal Society of Arts. He has organized investigations into the Borley Rectory hauntings; Langenhoe Church; The Queen's House at Greenwich; The Grenadier in Belgravia, London; Marble Arch; Eton Vicarage; Berry Pomeroy Castle in Devon; Newark Park in Gloucestershire; Glamis Castle in Scotland and Farnham Castle in Surrey.

During his career Peter has worked with many famous names, including mediums Eileen Garrett, Leslie Finch and Tom Corbett; researchers Muriel Hankey, Professor H.H. Price, Dr Oskar Goldberg and Mollie Goldney; and ghost enthusiasts Charles Chaplin, Michael Bentine, Sir John Gielgud, Sir Alec Guinness, Sir Ralph Richardson and Dennis Wheatley.

In 2000, Peter became Patron of The Ghost Research Foundation, which was founded by the author and Daniel Holmes in Oxford in 1992.

DOREEN VALIENTE
MOTHER OF MODERN WITCHCRAFT
4 January 1922–1 September 1999

Born in Mitcham, South London, on 4 January 1922 to Harry and Edith Dominy, Doreen Valiente was to be largely responsible for the revival of witchcraft and the creation of modern-day Wicca in Britain, her influence soon spreading around the world.

Her fascination with the haunted world around us was sparked at an early age when she saw, in her own words: 'What people would call the world of everyday reality as unreal, and saw behind it something that was very real and very potent. Just for a moment I had experienced what was beyond the physical. It was beautiful, wonderful, it wasn't frightening.' That experience, while watching the moon in a veiled sky one night during her early childhood, was to dictate the course of the rest of her life.

When Doreen was 13, her mother was having a terrible dispute with a colleague. Doreen asked her mother to obtain a sample of the woman's hair. Doreen performed a simple 'magic', and the woman left her mother alone. This success, although welcome, frightened her family and they sent Doreen to a convent school, which she hated, leaving on the day of her 15th birthday and vowing never to return. Throughout her teenage years her interest in the magical world grew as she immersed herself in the scant literature then available on the subject. She was influenced mostly by the works of Margaret Alice Murray and Charles Leland.

In 1941, aged 19, she was married for the first time, to Joanis Vlachopoulos, a 32-year-old merchant seaman. Six months later Doreen received word that he was lost at sea and presumed dead. She later moved to London where she was to meet her second husband. Casimiro Valiente was a refugee from the Spanish Civil War, and he met Doreen while recovering in London. The pair were married on 29 May 1944, and Doreen became Doreen Valiente.

Doreen and Casimiro moved to Bournemouth to be away from war-torn London and it was at this point in her life that her interest in the psychic side of life was rekindled. The Witchcraft Act was repealed in 1952 and shortly afterwards Doreen read an article in which the witch Cecil Williamson was discussing opening a Folklore Centre on the Isle of Man. The feature also mentioned a witches' coven which was operating in the Forest of Dean area – not far from where Doreen and Casimiro were living. She wrote to Cecil asking for information and Cecil passed her correspondence to Gerald Gardner – who had been initiated into the New Forest coven in 1939.

After a lengthy correspondence, Gerald arranged to meet up with Doreen at the home of a lady

BELOW: *Doreen Valiente, widely considered to be the 'mother of modern witchcraft', performs a magical rite.*

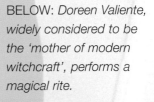

referred to as 'Dafo', in Christchurch. Dafo had first introduced Gerald to witchcraft, and the pair wished to assess Doreen's suitability for membership of the New Forest coven. Gerald gave her a copy of his book, *High Magic's Aid*, which she took away and read in earnest. A year later, in 1953, Gardner initiated her as a witch – giving her the witch name 'Ameth'.

Following her initiation, Doreen was allowed access to Gerald's own *Book of Shadows*– a record in which all rituals, spells and observations are recorded. She began to rewrite the material into a revised version which was to form the basis of Gardnerian Wicca – the most prominent strain of witchcraft in existence today. Gerald claimed that the book was the remnants of an old religion passed down through the centuries. But Doreen recognized elements from contemporary writers including the Gnostic Mass by the notorious Aleister Crowley (see pages 110–12) . She edited the content and added her own poetic flare to create the new edition.

By 1957 a rift had begun to form between Gerald and Doreen, now his High Priestess of the coven. A dispute arose over Gerald's persistent quest for publicity for their activities, and Doreen's wish to keep the coven secret and sacred. Doreen left Gerald's coven in 1957 to form her own with a fellow witch named Ned Grove. She would later restore her friendship with Gerald, but for now, her spiritual life had moved on.

In 1964, Doreen's mother, Edith, and Gerald both passed to the spirit world and she joined a new group – the coven with Ned Grove having disbanded by this time – who were following the '1735 Tradition' (a form of witchcraft that purports to include fragments of an ancient form of witchcraft). The coven was run by Robert Cochrane, but after being initially impressed, Doreen decided that Cochrane's group was not for her. Robert had tried to instigate a war against the followers of Gerald's Gardnerian Wicca, and Doreen strongly disapproved.

Following the death of Casimiro in 1972, Doreen devoted her time to writing, publishing *An ABC of Witchcraft* in 1973. It was followed in 1975 by *Natural Magic* and *Witchcraft for Tomorrow* in 1978. Doreen's original books are now sought-after and considered fundamental texts in Wiccan literature, and their publication led to her becoming consulted by other authors about their own works, many of which she contributed to and edited.

During the 1970s, Doreen spoke out against the government, which was planning to put new prohibitive witchcraft laws in place. She successfully lobbied the minister responsible and as a result, the new laws were scrapped. She lectured widely concerning witchcraft and Paganism, becoming the Patron of the Centre for Pagan Studies in 1995. The centre is run by John Belham-Payne, her last High Priest and witchcraft partner.

After spending her last years working enthusiastically for The Pagan Federation and numerous other groups to promote understanding of the craft, she passed peacefully on 1 September 1999. She bequeathed her enormous, unique archive to the Centre for Pagan Studies, including ritual items made for her by Gardner, as well as his original *Book of Shadows*, and her own. The books are considered to be modern witchcraft's most precious documents.

Before her passing, while struggling against cancer, she asked John Belham-Payne to publish the many poems that had been written over the years. The book, entitled *Charge of the Goddess*, published by Hexagon Hoopix, is a wonderful legacy to the witchcraft and Pagan community. Its inspired verse will no doubt be enjoyed by enthusiasts for many, many years to come.

It is impossible to measure Doreen's role in the creation of modern Wicca and the revival of interest in all forms of paganism in the latter half of the 20th century. Her enthusiasm, strength, kindness and depth mean that for those who knew her she is sorely missed, and for those that were never fortunate enough to have met her, like myself, she will always be remembered fondly as the Mother of Modern Witchcraft.

QUEEN VICTORIA

THE LONGEST REIGNING MONARCH IN BRITISH HISTORY
24 May 1819–22 January 1901

Victoria, who became queen in 1837, is at first glance not perhaps an obvious choice as a prominent figure of the paranormal. In fact, she had a deep interest in the supernatural, as is explored by Peter Underwood in his excellent work *Queen Victoria's Other World*.

Victoria was born at Kensington Palace on 24 May 1819, the sole daughter of Edward, Duke of Kent. On the death of King William IV in 1837, she inherited the throne at the tender age of 18. Throughout her life, even as a young child, she was a keen diarist and it is the content of these diaries, and anecdotes from her many associates, which point to a keen fascination with the supernatural world.

ABOVE: *Queen Victoria was fascinated by the unseen, and allegedly befriended the medium Robert Lees.*

As England's longest-reigning monarch – her reign lasted nearly 64 years – she is fondly remembered as a strong, confident woman, much loved by her people. But her hidden fascination with the macabre is not well known. Peter Underwood has suggested that this facet of her character has been intentionally overlooked by other members of the British royal family.

Throughout her childhood, Victoria is known to have sought out places where she might hear ghost stories, and visited haunted buildings whenever possible. One of her favourites was The Royal Anchor – an inn at Liphook in Hampshire, reputed to be haunted by the phantom of a highwayman named Captain Jacques. She is known to have returned there at a later date with her husband Prince Albert, whom she married in 1840. Albert shared her interest in the occult world, and joined the young Victoria on long walks during which they would discuss the afterlife and all its possibilities. After one such walk Victoria wrote to her eldest daughter 'I feel now to be so acquainted with death – and to be so much nearer that unseen world'.

In 1845, following the birth of nine children, Queen Victoria commissioned a mansion on the Isle of Wight which she named Osborne House. It was to be her perfect retreat. One source has suggested that Victoria and Albert experimented with a talking board at Osborne House and witnessed a moving table as a result.

ABOVE: *Queen Victoria had a profound interest in the ghostly heritage of Britain, often visiting sites with haunted histories.*

One of Victoria's closest acquaintances during her later life was said to be the medium Robert Lees, although this is a controversial claim, still disputed by many. In his book *When Dead Kings Speak*, published in 1985, author Tony Ortzen revisited the apparent link between Spiritualism and Queen Victoria. Research has shown that accounts of the Queen's interest in the spirit world are consistent in substance and content wherever they have been published. Robert Lee's daughter has stated that Victoria summoned her father on at least six different occasions in order to attempt to contact the Prince Consort following his death in 1861.

In 1897, Victoria knighted Sir William Crookes. Crookes was a prominent investigator of the psychic world and President of the Society for Psychical Research. He was also Chairman of the original Ghost Club and a fellow of the Royal Society; he was later awarded the Order of Merit in 1910.

At the end of his life, Prince Albert told the Queen: 'We don't know in what state we shall meet again; but that we shall recognize each other and be together in eternity I am perfectly certain'. In an end befitting a beloved monarch, Victoria died at her favourite residence,

Osborne House, on 22 January 1901. Perhaps her soul was rekindled with Albert, her one and only love, or perhaps, as some say, her ghost still walks the earth at Osborne House, the place where she spent so many happy times.

According to author Sir Simon Marsden, who wrote about Queen Victoria in his book entitled *This Spectred Isle*, a strange, inexplicable odor of orange blossom and jasmine – the mixture believed to have been the Queen's favourite scent during her lifetime – is often noticed in what was formerly her bedroom.

LEFT: *Sir William Crookes, one-time President of the Society for Psychical Research, was knighted by Queen Victoria.*

Chapter 6

The Modern World of the Paranormal

We live in a scientific world, where fact and faith do not mix. Belief in the haunted realm, and scientific reliance on proof of that world, are poles apart, and despite more than a century of serious psychical research, the truth is that there is still no scientifically verifiable answer to the question of whether a spirit world exists or not.

In an increasingly technological age, is there still a place for the supernatural in our lives? As science tells us that things do not exist, do we accept that final statement, or do we linger with the 'might be, may be', because the possibility of something beyond the material world excites us? Today, our fascination with the supernatural and paranormal seems stronger than ever, as the box-office success of the films of M. Night Shyalaman (*The Sixth Sense*, *Signs*, etc.) testifies. The American TV series 'Medium', loosely based on the crimes that psychic Allison Dubois has helped law-enforcement agencies to solve, is screened in over a dozen countries around the world.

In this chapter we will take a look at some modern accounts of the supernatural using contemporary evidence caught with modern devices. Ghosts and spirits still seem to infiltrate our popular culture, manifesting now not only in ancient historic halls, but on celluloid and even for sale via eBay!

Some parapsychologists and ghost hunters believe they are on the verge of a major paranormal revelation, where the combined forces of science and the psychic will meet. The 21st century will, I am sure, provide many answers to things we do not currently understand, but with those answers of course come even more questions. For now, let us take a tour around the modern world of the paranormal.

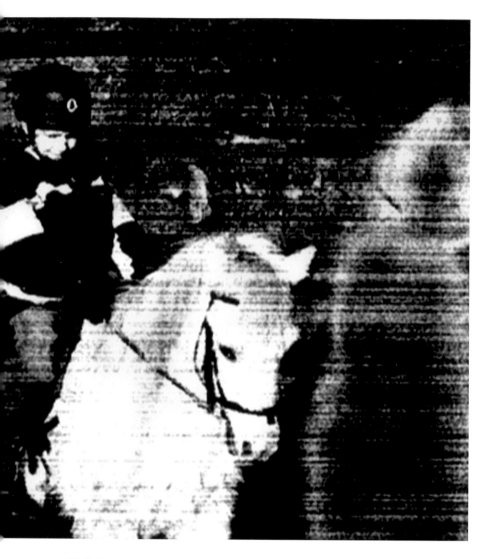

THE HAUNTED MÉNAGE
Summer 1985

It was at Cobham Manor Riding School near Maidstone in Kent that, one summer evening in 1985, Janet and Martin Emmott caught a ghost on their home video camera. This footage has been the talk of the paranormal community, and their dinner table, ever since. It was the first time in 20 years that Janet had ridden a horse. Having been a keen equestrian in her teenage years but not having ridden since, she decided to join her daughter in the ménage for a canter. Martin had come along to watch the pair enjoying themselves and had brought along his family video camera to record the event, but what he caught was not merely his wife and daughter, but also the solitary spectre of a 17th-century pilgrim.

The footage lay in the camera overnight unwatched until the following day, when Janet decided to take a look. As she watched herself and her daughter trotting around the ménage on their horses, something caught her eye. She stopped the tape and wound it back, astounded by what she had seen. There in the background, apparently right next to the horses, stood a tall man with long grey hair and a white cravat dressed in long black robes! Who he was and how he had appeared was a mystery to Janet who, being a police officer, was used to hard facts and not remotely partial to flights of fancy. The figure had not been there at the time, yet there he was for all to see on the tape. When Martin called her later that evening she exclaimed that they had a ghost on the tape – he thought she was joking until he returned home to see for himself.

From examining the history of the riding school, and more particularly the ménage, it turns out that it lies very close to the ancient Pilgrim's Way – a track used by pilgrims journeying to Canterbury to see the last resting place of St Thomas à Becket. Could this strange figure be a vision from the past, a pilgrim making his way from Winchester to Canterbury? It seemed unlikely, and Martin wanted a professional opinion, so he took the tape to his local television studio.

Rather than quash the ghostly theory, the engineers only compounded it, telling him that it was definitely a figure and not a trick of the light – but that if he examined the tape more closely he would see the 'head' of the ghost emerging from the ground when he had filmed that part of the ménage moments earlier!

I have watched the footage and it certainly sends a shiver down your spine to see the motionless figure silently observing the riders as they trot, obliviously, around the ménage. Janet, Martin and their daughter are certain there was no-one in the vicinity at the time and remain convinced, as do many others, that what they captured on film is a ghost.

ABOVE: A ghostly 17th-century pilgrim was caught on video in Kent during the summer of 1985.

PREVIOUS PAGE: Ancient places still hold onto the ghosts of the past despite arguments, based on 21st-century technology, that they do not exist.

THREE MEN AND A BABY – AND A GHOST!
1987

Films with a paranormal theme have always been surrounded by urban myths, untruths and a general air of unease, which of course is exactly what the producers of big budget blockbusters want – publicity. But what if a ghost appears in your film – even though it has no paranormal plotline? Such was the case with *Three Men and a Baby*, produced by Touchstone Pictures in 1987 – the tale of three unmarried men bringing up a child. After the movie was released, rumours began to circulate about a ghost that had appeared unnoticed by the editors in a scene filmed in a supposedly haunted location.

People began to pause the film at the indicated scene to 'see' the ghost, and sure enough – there it was. The figure of a small boy peers through the drapes of an apartment during a scene in which actor Ted Danson and actress Celeste Holm are walking through the room.

Stories followed to explain this weird phenomenon, with a tale that the boy had committed suicide in the apartment using a shotgun to blow his brains out becoming most popular. The inspiration for this version was an amorphous black shape which is visible in the film scene and which resembles the outline of a shotgun, this being created by the effect of a white drape in front of the boy's black clothing – but this was far from the truth.

Other rumours elaborate further, telling how the dead boy's parents fled the house after his death, selling it to movie producers to use as a film location. One version even went on to say that following the film's release, and the 'appearance' of her son's ghost, the mother tried to sue the production company after they refused to delete the scene.

In actuality, none of this occurred. The scene in question was shot on a soundstage in a studio in Toronto; it was not a 'real' location – and not a haunted one either. The 'boy' was in fact a 'standee' – a cardboard cut-out – created by the props department to further enhance the storyline of Ted Danson's character being a failed actor. His character was so vain that he had a blown-up picture of himself in the apartment. In the original script several references to this prop were made, but these were cut from the final version, resulting in the urban myth of a ghost in the film.

The case of *Three Men and a Baby* is a good example of how we react to claims of the supernatural, especially when it comes to 'proof' captured on film – 'the camera doesn't lie', supposedly. With televison programmes currenty exploring the paranormal all over the world, and with a resurgence in paranormal and horror films, it is not surprising that these tales develop. What is equally unsurprising is the fact that most of these entertainment-based shows have little or no basis in fact, the emphasis being on thrilling the audience rather than on educating them. A conflict is thus created between the spiritual and the greedy, one side exploiting the haunted world in a profit-making exercise, thus debasing and misrepresenting a field of investigation that others take very seriously. Controversy and accusations of fraud abound within these television productions and films. In a world where profit counts, there is no room for the truth – the unseen world will not 'deliver on demand', it seems.

BELOW: *A ghostly 'extra' in the film* Three Men and a Baby *was nothing more than a prop cut-out.*

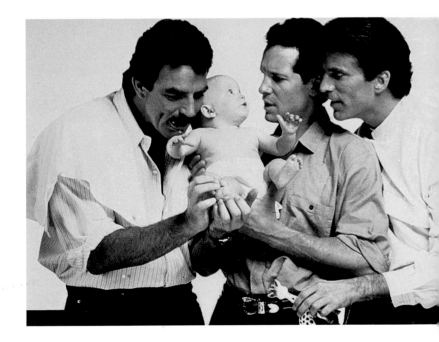

THE CURSE OF THE POLTERGEIST FILMS

1980s–Present day?

Urban myths have haunted other major film productions, including the *Poltergeist* films written and produced by Steven Spielberg in the 1980s. The myth alleges that the casts of all the films were cursed because of a real skeleton which was used as a prop in the first film. Actress Jo Beth Williams has added to this story by pointing out in various interviews

RIGHT: *Unsurprisingly, urban myths, such as the 'curse' of the film* Poltergeist, *tend to spring up around horror films.*

that she was told the bones used in a swimming pool scene were real.

The 'curse' story evolved from the fact that four of the films' stars and one producer have suffered premature or mysterious deaths. The actors and actresses who are said to have died at the hands of the curse include: Dominique Dunne, from the first *Poltergeist* film, who was strangled by a jealous lover in 1982; Heather O'Rourke, who played Carol Anne in all three movies, who died in 1988 after going into septic shock; Julian Beck, who played the evil 'Kane' in *Poltergeist 2*, who died of stomach cancer (although he had already been diagnosed with this before being approached to play a role in the film); and Will Sampson, who played The Medicine Man in *Poltergeist 2*, who died from kidney failure. Brian Gibson, who directed *Poltergeist 2*, also died prematurely from Ewing's Sarcoma in 2004.

Another interesting incident linked with the *Poltergeist* trilogy occurred during a photo shoot featuring Zelda Rubenstein who played the psychic. In one picture her face is entirely obscured by a shining white light; strangely, the picture was being taken at the same moment as her mother's death thousands of miles away.

In the past few years a television series entitled *Poltergeist: The Legacy* has been running on American networks and has now been released on DVD. Time will tell whether the curse of *Poltergeist* has crossed from the big screen to the cable networks, or whether the film's tragic heritage is finally over.

ABOVE: *Mysterious deaths of the cast and crew of the* Poltergeist *films have resulted in a theory that the productions were affected by malevolent supernatural influences.*

THE SCOLE EXPERIMENT – MODERN EVIDENCE OF A HAUNTED WORLD?

1993–1998

Considered by many to have produced the best evidence of the existence of life after death, The Scole Experiment was a series of séances conducted by a group of sitters over a four-year period in which a variety of visual, audible and physical phenomena were witnessed under controlled conditions. The results of the research, and experiences reported, were compiled by Grant and Jane Solomon from original recordings made by the sitters and published in their book *The Scole Experiment* in 1999.

The story began in a small farmhouse in Scole, Norfolk – the home of physical mediums John and Sandra Foy. (Physical mediums are those whose physical appearance changes temporarily while they are communing with spirits.) The Foys had recently moved to the area and wished to form their own psychic development group, bringing some members from a group they had been previously involved with in Postwick, Norfolk. The Foys were well known throughout the Spiritualist community, having founded The Noah's Ark Society – a national body which helps developing mediums move into physical mediumship. Robin had been urged to start the society after a spirit named Noah Zerdin had spoken to him during a sitting in 1990.

ABOVE: *A shape resembling a human head appeared on film during an experiment in 1998.*

The Foys' new home was a farmhouse with a small cellar, which was perfect to conduct the sittings in as they would be able to ensure that no light would seep in – and they nicknamed it 'the Scole hole'. Over the first few weeks different people took part in trying to raise the spirits in the darkened cellar, but to no avail. After several changes in the group some small activity began to take place – contact had been made.

Over a period of weeks, several discarnate entities made their presence known to the Scole Group. These included a 'gatekeeper' named Manu, a charity worker from Oxford named Emily Bradshaw, an Indian Prince named Raji, and a Guinness-loving priest named Patrick McKenna. Together the spirit team were able to produce flashing lights, splashing water, voices and *apports* – items which would materialize in the room.

With the strength of the phenomena increasing, the Scole Group invited guests to witness the activity, and sometimes as many as 25 people would watch in awe as lights danced and flew around the cellar, making contact with the sitters and giving them a small electric shock.

The Scole Group realized early on that what they were achieving had not been done in such a successful way before, and they wanted to ensure that it was properly authenticated and recorded, so they contacted the oldest and most respected of psychic research bodies in the

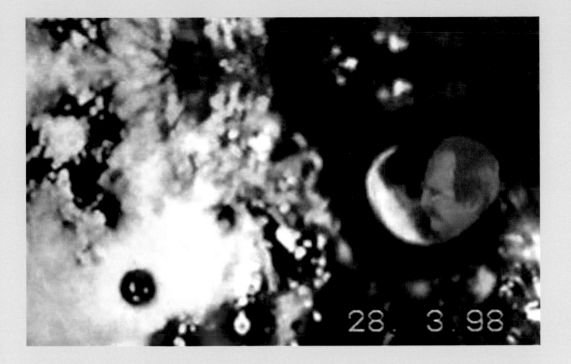

UK – The Society for Psychical Research. The SPR sent three noted investigators to examine the claims made by the Scole Group and they observed the sittings over a period of two years. At the end of their research, the SPR members concluded that they had not found any evidence of deception or fraud, and published a 300-page report detailing their findings.

One of the most peculiar phenomena produced by the spirits was the manifestation of images from around the world – and allegedly from their own 'spirit world' – onto factory-sealed camera films which were placed in the midst of the sitters during the séances and then later developed without having been opened by the group. Images, purported to be of alternative worlds and layers of existence, were later recorded on video cameras as well as on photographic films – the pictures psychically imprinted on the tapes by the spirit team working from the 'other side'.

After travelling to six different countries – Ireland, Spain, the USA, Switzerland, Germany and the Netherlands – to conduct sittings with other psychics and mediums, achieving results in every case, the Scole Group's research came to an end on 23 November 1998. A message was received from a spirit communicator which explained that the Scole Group would be unable to contact the same spirit team again as they had been 'moved on'. The reason given was that their communications had created a problem in space time with an 'interdimensional doorway' which had been created to conduct the research at Scole. A researcher from the future with malevolent intentions had discovered a way to intercept the doorway and as a result it was shut down.

Following the end of The Scole Experiment, and the subsequent publication of the book, the case became mired in controversy. Various points were made by skeptics about protocols which were not observed during all of the experiments and sittings, and doubt was cast over much of the evidence presented.

Those involved have always asserted that their experience was genuine and credible, and taken at face-value it is probably the best evidence of intelligent survival beyond bodily death that the world has ever known. The research continues throughout the world as others have followed the principles set out in the book, forming their own groups and, according to websites, finding that they have been able to replicate some of the phenomena experienced by the Scole Group, and contact their own spirit teams.

THE BELGRAVE HALL 'GHOST'

23 December 1998

Belgrave Hall, a large townhouse in Leicester, was built by Edmund Craddock at the beginning of the 18th century as a private home for his family. Over the centuries it has swapped hands several times and in 1936 the local council converted the house into a museum chronicling its history. It is said to be haunted by several spectres, which flit among the shadows in the walled garden and along deserted corridors of the building.

Former curator Stuart Warburton is on record as saying, 'The Hall is haunted, there is no question about that', while Michael Snuggs, who works as head gardener at the Hall, has sighted a phantom lady in a terracotta-coloured gown staring at him from behind the glass panes of a window in the house. He said that the spectre smiled at him before turning and walking out of view.

Other sightings include that of a 'Grey Lady' and a 'Green Lady', although critics suggest these may all be the same spirit, described in different ways as a result of the differing lighting conditions in which they have been witnessed. Another ghostly phenomenon is the gentle scent of cooking which wafts through the Hall. Stewed fruit and baking bread has been commented on by staff and visitors, despite the fact that there is no working kitchen in the house today.

The Hall is now famous throughout the haunted world following the appearance of one of its ghosts on a CCTV security camera. The image, which appears to show one, or possibly two, shiny white figures standing outside a bay window of the Hall, was caught at 4.48am on the morning of 23 December 1998. The security camera system which observes the grounds of the mansion was triggered into action, caught the image and then 'froze' for no apparent reason, before returning to normal. Adding to the mystery, a rolling mist of white substance is seen moving swiftly along the wall and out of vision in the footage caught immediately after the camera resumed functioning.

RIGHT: *Belgrave Hall in Leicester has been the scene of hauntings for many years.*

The national media was immediately alerted, pending a full paranormal investigation, and news that a ghost had been caught on film travelled around the world on various national television networks. The immediate assumption was that one of the spirits on camera was the 'Victorian Lady' who is known to haunt the mansion. She is thought to be the wandering ghost of Charlotte Ellis, daughter of former local MP John Ellis, whose family once lived at the Hall. The rolling mist was described as 'ectoplasm', indicating that the spirits had dissipated and moved away in an ethereal, mist-like form. But proof had yet to enter the equation.

The International Society for Paranormal Research (ISPR) was called in to investigate. A team of field investigators from across the USA, led by parapsychologist Dr Larry Montz and psychic Daena Smoller, descended on the Hall.

The team identified several different entities inside the Hall, including a strong male presence which was so powerful they fled the room, believing the entity capable of causing harm. Another spirit was that of a small child who had died of tuberculosis, a third was of a man who had fallen to his death down the stairs. All this information was obtained psychically. Many of the spirits highlighted by the ISPR were later verified by council records that showed that people fitting these descriptions had indeed lived in the house. But they did not find any trace of paranormal activity in the area where the glowing white figures had been caught by the CCTV video camera. Was this particular 'ghost' nothing more than a trick of the light?

After months of research by various paranormal investigators, the paranormal community is still divided as to the validity of the Belgrave Hall video 'ghost'. Some see it as further proof that spirits exist, while others claim this is an environmental phenomenon, perhaps that of a leaf or ingress of water which had reflected a light source. What is not so easy to explain is the fog-like substance which moves across the wall just after the spirits disappear – another piece of credible evidence according to those that believe – while the skeptics see it as just that – fog!

THE HAUNTED WORLD HITS THE PROPERTY MARKET
From 2000

Does having a ghost affect the value of your property? This is a question often asked but never adequately answered – until now. A recent report was commissioned by Lloyds TSB to try and discover if having a phantasmal heritage would affect the potential sale of a house. Remarkably, it does.

With the ever-continuing interest in paranormal television and films, shows such as ITV's *Haunted Homes* and UKTV's *Ghost Detectives* appear to be spooking buyers of older properties. Over half of the people interviewed for the report said they believed in ghosts and would not buy a house if they thought they might be sharing it with an undead companion. A further 39 per cent admitted that knowing someone had died in the property might put them off buying, and being located near to a burial site would make almost half think twice before putting in an offer.

Even Britain's Royal family have been affected, with Nether Lypiatt Manor – home of Prince and Princess Michael of Kent – being reduced in price by £500,000 during a recent sale. *Psychic News*, the weekly British newspaper of the paranormal, speculated that the reason for the drop in asking price could be attributable to the many spirits that are said to inhabit the Gloucestershire pile.

Set in 14.5 hectares (36 acres) of wonderful countryside, the Grade I listed mansion was built in 1703 for Judge Charles Coxe. In a feature published by *The Sunday Times,* the reporter wrote 'The story has it that Coxe sentenced one of the ironsmiths who worked on

BELOW: Nether Lypiatt Manor – a royal home haunted by the shades of the past.

the elaborate front gate to be hanged for some crime, but only after waiting until he had finished the job'. The house has allegedly been haunted by the ironsmith's spirit ever since. Another tale involves a former owner who committed murder to acquire funds to buy the house. The building is said to have been exorcised several times, and one famous guitarist who stayed at the mansion fled during the middle of the night, asking for his luggage to be sent on later.

Christopher Dewe, an estate agent working for Knight Frank in Oxford, was quoted in an article published by *The Daily Telegraph* newspaper in August 2005 as follows:

When haunted houses cause a lot of problems with viewings, then one has to suggest to sellers that an exorcism might be a sensible option, otherwise we don't tend to mention it. There was once a house where a bolt on a door would always slam locked if you closed it, so we were told never to close the door. Once I forgot and I have never seen a viewer run so quickly out of a house in my life!

Selling stigmatized property comes with its own problems, as is highlighted in the case of Lowes Cottage (see pages 54–7). A vendor might now find that they are in breach of contract for not disclosing any known history of hauntings in a house, even if it is purely anecdotal. But whether the presence of a ghost, something which is a matter of personal belief and not 'science' (not yet, anyway), could be proven in a court of modern law is something yet to be discovered. The 'proof' may not be necessary, however, as the psychological impact of the possibility of a haunting would in itself be enough to 'spook' potential buyers and affect any new owners on a long-term basis. Thus, the reality of the ghost is no longer important; society's reaction to the possibility is.

ABOVE TOP AND BOTTOM: *Houses with a spectral heritage generally take longer to sell nowadays thanks to mass media focus on all things paranormal.*

TRACY RETURNS FROM THE GRAVE?

July 2002

In July 2002, a sequence of video caught at a wrecker service station in Oklahoma, USA, made its debut in the haunted world – purportedly showing a ghost walking around a car lot. The footage became known as 'The Pucketts Ghost' because it was captured by a security surveillance camera at Pucketts Wrecker Station, part of which is used to store vehicles which have been involved in serious collisions. What is strange about this particular ghost claim is that after the film was released, a family came forward and identified the spirit as a deceased relative.

Interestingly, at the time it was being recorded on video, the ghost was also seen by a staff member named Kathy Henley, who happened to be watching the camera monitor as the spirit moved around the yard. Kathy asked a colleague to go and check whether there was anyone around which might explain what she had seen, but on going out there was no-one there.

The Martin family, who contacted the television station who first showed the footage to the nation, believe the spirit is that of Tracy Martin, their daughter, who had died from injuries in a car accident on 30 June that year. The remains of the car in which Tracy had been travelling had been stored pending an insurance investigation at the yard, and had been removed just hours before the images where caught.

In a bizarre twist, the figure appears to be wearing overalls in the CCTV footage – Tracy's clothing of choice, according to a family portrait. Her family were reported by *Newschannel 4* as saying that they were not surprised that she had 'come back' to let them know she was OK, as she always did things in grand style.

Paranormal researchers who claim to have investigated the case say that they managed to recreate a similar effect using a toy action figure which they animated using a string, thus throwing the usual doubts on these 'ghost on film' claims.

BELOW: *A ghost was seen on film at a petrol station in Oklahoma in July 2002.*

GEORGE'S GHOSTLY ARM

September 2003

It was the discovery of two cans of beer on the floor at a Co-Op supermarket in the Cornish town of Penzance in September 2003 which sparked an investigation into how they got there – resulting in the national media broadcasting the footage from the shop's security camera to the nation. When playing back the tape to see how the cans had arrived on the floor, staff at the shop were amazed to see a grey, skeletal arm emerge out of the shelf and proceed to push the beer cans onto the floor. The tape made national news and GMTV sent a reporter and medium to look at the incident in more detail.

When psychic medium Emma Schofield entered the premises she sensed the presence of a very strong male entity, which she described as 'wanting to keep his business quiet and needing to have some fun'. Perhaps this was the male ghost (nicknamed George) that has been noted by staff and duty managers working alone in the store – they have heard thunderous footsteps ascending and descending the staircase which leads to a warehouse on an upper floor. On other occasions doors have opened or closed of their own accord, sometimes slamming in the face of those who approach them. Store worker Avril O'Leary related the following:

Three of us were working that night and we were shutting our tills when we noticed cans of Stella [beer] all spilt on the floor, some distance from the shelf. We looked at the CCTV and it was as if they had been pushed off the shelf by something. You can just make out an arm on the video.

Avril described how poltergeist activity had been observed in the warehouse and said that she had also seen the building's second spirit – that of a gentler ghost she and her colleagues had named 'Mary'. One day as she was working stacking boxes, Avril turned around to see a grey figure standing a few feet away from her, but in a few moments she vanished. She said 'It doesn't unnerve me at all, I find it fascinating'.

Critics have said this is a plain hoax, merely someone pushing the cans from the other side of the shelves, but that is impossible as the shelf unit stands flush against an exterior wall – there is no room for anyone to stand behind the shelf. The mystery was compounded further when GMTV tried to send the images from the video tape to their London headquarters in preparation for the transmission – the video tape snapped unexpectedly in two.

Paranormal expert Ian Addicoat of the South West Paranormal Research Organization told the *Western Morning News*, who carried the story on 19 September 2003, that he was not entirely convinced that it was a genuine ghost on film:

We were asked to look at the tape a while ago and there is one second missing from the timing. The time on the tape is constant until the crucial moment, when the beer comes off the shelf, then it jumps. The cans go straight from the shelf and then appear on the floor. I am not suggesting it is a hoax because it is quite possible that the place is haunted, but the tape worries me and we would need to do more research.

BELOW: *A CCTV camera in the Co-Op at Penzance caught a strange image of a spectral arm in 2003.*

THE HAMPTON COURT GHOST

19 December 2003

Hampton Court Palace, on the banks of the River Thames, 16 kilometres (10 miles) from central London, England, catapulted into the news in December 2003 after an astonishing piece of CCTV footage showing a robed figure tampering with a pair of fire doors came to light. The footage, which was shown on television networks throughout the world, clearly shows a tall figure wearing a dark hooded gown with a cord around his middle shutting a double fire door, which is situated in a part of the palace where the public and costumed guides do not go. Beneath the cowl a face can be seen – palace security guard James Faukes said 'It was incredibly spooky because the face just didn't look human'.

The case began with a security alarm sounding, indicating that a fire door had been opened. Staff hurried to the doors, but were perplexed to find them closed and no-one around to explain how the alarm had been triggered. It was only later when they played back the footage of the doors in question that the spooky figure was revealed. The doors pop open apparently of their own accord, and then the ghostly figure comes into view to slam them shut again. Security records also showed that the same alarm sounded the day before, at the same time – 1pm – and also the day after the ghost was caught on CCTV, again at the same time. However, 'he' has only been caught on tape on one of these three occasions.

The CCTV footage of the ghost closing the fire doors has baffled researchers of the paranormal, including noted parapsychologist Richard Wiseman, who was quoted in *The Daily Mail* saying, 'It could be the best ghost sighting ever, I haven't seen anything that would match that at all.' When asked if it was a publicity stunt to attract more visitors with an interest in the spectral heritage of the palace, Vikki Wood, a spokesperson for the tourist attraction said 'It's not a joke, we haven't manufactured it. We genuinely don't know who or what it is.'

The palace is well known as a haunted building, with numerous wraiths flitting among the shadows, the most famous being that of Catherine Howard who was charged with adultery in 1541 by her husband, King Henry VIII. After being placed under arrest, she escaped and fled wailing along a corridor now known as The Haunted Gallery to plead for her life, but she was dragged back and later executed. The psychic imprint of this terrible situation can still be felt today and her ghost has been seen racing along the gallery on many occasions.

Other apparitions which have been reported in the past include Sibell Penn, who was buried at the Palace in 1562. After her tomb was disturbed in 1829 during some building work, an unexplained whirring sound was heard echoing through the southwest wing. When workers traced the sound back to a brick wall they uncovered a secret

BELOW: *Hampton Court Palace, a celebrated haunted house in Surrey.*

room in which was contained an old spinning wheel – just like the one Penn used to use. Another active spirit is that of Jane Seymour, third wife of Henry VIII, whose melancholic wraith glides around the cobbled courtyards on moonlit evenings, carrying a glowing candle to light her way.

Ghostly sightings are commonplace for visitors and tourists who soak up the ancient atmosphere of the magnificent building, which is known as one of the most haunted places in the country.

BELOW: *Hampton Court's latest ghost – that of a habit-clad figure – caught by a security camera in 2003.*

THE DEMON BOX
February 2004

ABOVE: *An impish demon known as a 'Dybbuk' was thought to inhabit a box sold on eBay in 2004.*

OPPOSITE: *Fragments believed to be of a gravestone were included in the demonic lot offered for sale.*

On 9 February 2004, a wine cabinet was acquired by a new owner, having been sold through the Internet auction site eBay. After a furious bidding war in which over 25,000 hits were made, in the last few minutes, the winner was Jason Haxton, the curator of a museum of curiosities, who wished to add the box to his collection. According to the description on eBay, the box was inhabited by a Dybbuk – a Jewish demon which brought harm upon those who possessed the box.

When opened, it was found to contain various artefacts, including two locks of hair, a penny, a dried rose bud, a wine goblet, a candlestick with octopus legs and a section of granite from a gravestone on which was engraved the word 'Shalom' in Hebrew.

The seller of the item had been told by the previous owner (both of whom wish to remain anonymous) that it was 'haunted' and that he was glad to be rid of it. He claimed that since owning the box, which he had bought at an estate sale, a variety of strange occurrences had befallen him, including the smell of cat urine around his house and the unexplained smashing of light bulbs. His original intention had been to give the box as a birthday gift to his mother, and after storing it temporarily in his shop basement, where the phenomena had been witnessed, he presented it to her on 31 October (Hallowe'en). The story goes that after leaving her alone with the box to make a telephone call he was summoned back as she had suffered a stroke out of the blue, later spelling out 'HATE GIFT' and 'NO GIFT' using an alphabet board while in hospital.

The account written on eBay to accompany pictures of the box and contents explained how the box was subsequently given to the seller's sister for a short time, before being returned and causing him to lose his hair, until eventually, blaming it for the afflictions that had struck his family, he decided to sell it on. As soon as it was featured on the auction site, emails began circulating in the paranormal community – interest was great, and many had been intrigued by the legend of the box and its possible haunting by an evil spirit.

Whether it was an elaborate hoax, reaping a rich reward for a box of junk, or a real paranormal artefact which should be treated with kid gloves, the Dybbuk box has now entered the annals of haunted history. The new owner, Jason Haxton, corresponded for some time with Paul Howse, president of The Ghost Research Foundation, after buying the box. He told Paul that despite not accepting the story related via its last owner, he was not taking any chances, and was planning to place the box in storage until he could investigate the claim further.

RIGHT: *The haunted wine cabinet contained cryptic Hebrew text.*

Conclusion

MODERN RESEARCH METHODS AND PARAPSYCHOLOGY

Advances in the contemporary investigation of the unseen world have increased dramatically since the last decade of the 20th century. Gaussmeters, elaborate temperature gauges and computers have replaced notebooks, compasses and Ouija boards, with the modern ghost hunter working with academic organizations to try and explain those areas of human experience that remain unexplained.

The development of parapsychology, once a pseudoscience, has now reached the level where it is recognized by several academic bodies in the UK. Led by the Koestler Parapsychology Unit at Edinburgh University, many other universities have now followed suit and are offering courses and conducting research into the wide field of the paranormal. The lay researcher has also stepped into the scientific arena with much less emphasis on personal

observations and more focus on evidence recorded by instruments.

In the USA, the Parapsychology Foundation, which was founded by medium Eileen J. Garrett and the Honourable Frances P. Bolton in 1951, is now a one-stop-shop for both academic and lay researchers around the world. The organization is a not-for-profit corporation which offers grants and advice to further the serious study of the haunted world. Acting as a forum for discussion, a publisher of various journals, and a central library offering the public the chance to peruse a vast collection of material collected over the past 50 years, the Parapsychology Foundation is now a beacon in the world of international research into supernatural experiences of all kinds.

In the UK, leading researchers are delving deeper into the subconscious and conscious mind, investigating how the environment affects the way we perceive the world around us. Investigations into atoms and alternative realities in quantum physics are now explored alongside the more traditional enquiries into haunted houses. The dark creepy castle has been replaced in many instances by the laboratory, with experimentation focussed more on the human mind and less on the 'haunted' environment.

Living in an ever-advancing technological world the questions which our forefathers were unable to explain are now being answered by science, but these answers, rather than putting an end to the matter, are themselves raising more and more questions – ensuring fertile ground for the parapsychologists, ghost hunters and lay researchers for many years to come.

LEFT: *Ghostly tales will always prevail, despite the world moving into a more technologically advanced age.*

GLOSSARY

APPARITION
A Stage 4 manifestation that is sometimes, but not always, visible to the human eye.

BLACK STREAM
A ley line of negative influence. Black streams absorb and exude negative feelings and vibrations, and can induce illness, headaches, depression and degenerative diseases. Black streams can be reversed by the use of crystals and by some psychics and mediums. They attract negative entities and are often linked to the presence and creation of elemental ghosts.

CASPER EFFECT
The appearance of wispy, transparent or translucent Stage 1 ghosts in photographs or video film, so-called because of its similarity in appearance to the fictional ghost character 'Casper, the friendly ghost'.

CLAIRAUDIENT
A medium or psychic who receives information from the other side in the form of sounds.

CLAIRSENTIENT
A medium who receives information from the other side by experiencing feelings, including physical ones.

CLAIRVOYANT
A medium who receives information from the other side by 'feeling' information, and relays it in one's own words.

DEMATERIALIZATION
The dissipation of a materialization, i.e. when a ghost vanishes or disappears.

ECTOPLASM
A sub-physical substance that can sometimes be seen with the naked eye. The word originates from the Greek 'ektos' and 'plasma' meaning 'exteriorized substance'. The structure of a ghost is believed to be made up of ectoplasm, and it apparently takes form in our physical world by manipulating energies such as electricity and human energy. The more energy available, the more physically 'real' the ghost becomes, until it is a complete manifestation.

ELECTRONIC VOICE PHENOMENA (EVP)
A recording of voices of the dead that occurs at a frequency not audible by the human ear.

ELEMENTAL GHOST
A non-human ghost form that exists on a lower level of existence than other ghost types. Elemental ghosts are an embodiment of the actions and intents that have taken place in the ghost's haunting ground. They have limited intelligence and are thought to be created by extreme positive or negative energy that is put into a location over a long period of time. Elemental ghosts can be created by occult ritual; extremes of intent (good or evil) by humans in the location; actions, experiences and emotions that take place at the location, such as murder, suffering, happiness, love and hate.

ESP
Extra Sensory Perception is a power beyond the normal five senses.

ETHER
The fifth element, thought to permeate all space. Ether is believed to be the only element conducive to ectoplasm formation. The acceptance of the existence of ether could help explain why some psychic manifestations appear 'out of thin air' or in apparent levitation and not resting or standing on anything solid. These ghost manifestations are manipulating the ether as a source of stability.

EXORCISM
The ritual of dispersing a ghost from a location or person, usually against its will. Appointed exorcists of various faiths, especially the Roman Catholic faith, normally conduct these rituals. It is a fact that, even today, every diocese in Britain has its own appointed exorcist, although the Church keeps this area of its work closely guarded.

GENIUS LOCI

The 'spirit' of a place. This can be affected by the people who live in the place; by ley-line orientation (positive or negative); by events that occur in the place, such as murder or extreme suffering; and by other inputs of positive or negative influence.

GHOST HIGHWAY

A term for a ley line that is used to explain how ghost entities travel from one place to another, in the same way that we use roads; also known as ghost paths.

GHOSTPRINT

A handprint left in flour or dust by a spectre.

GHOST RESCUE

The work of psychics or mediums who apparently release entities from the ghost realm and help them reach the afterworld. Similar to exorcism, except that techniques used in ghost rescue are more gentle and kind, as ghost rescue takes into account the wishes and feelings of the ghost, whereas exorcism does not.

GHOSTSTEP

A footprint left in flour or dust by a spectre.

JINX FACTOR

Locations subject to the 'jinx factor' bring about camera malfunctions, video equipment jamming or inexplicable interference by supernatural agencies to reclaim photographic or video evidence of their existence. For example, a photograph of a ghost goes missing, a processed camera film is blank or a video tape of ghost phenomena wipes itself clean for no reason.

KHU

An ancient Egyptian word for a ghost.

LEY LINE

A straight line of aligned landmarks (such as tors, rocky outcrops or hills) occurring naturally in the landscape, along which flows an unknown force, possibly related to electromagnetism. These occur naturally, but nearly always include additional sites built by man, such as castles or churches. They normally have spiritual or ritualistic importance, and include megalithic monuments, burial mounds and historic buildings.

MANES

A general term used by the Romans to describe ghosts.

MATERIALIZATION

A Stage 4 manifestation that has enough energy to become physically real in the living world.

MEDIUM

Someone who is sensitive to ghosts, and is unusually receptive to them. Some mediums relay messages, supposedly from the other side; others use their power to aid psychic investigations. Most mediums have the ability to become temporarily possessed by a ghost and to allow the ghost to speak through them.

ORB

A commonly used term for a Stage 1 energy genesis.

OTHER SIDE

In many beliefs, the 'other side' is the place where spirits go when the body dies. In broader terms, it is also used to describe a place where anything believed to remain after death exists. Also known as the afterworld.

OUIJA BOARD

A circular board with the letters of the alphabet on it that sometimes also contains key words, such as 'Yes' and 'No'. Ouija boards are used to contact the spirits of the dead, who supposedly spell out messages to the living by moving an upturned glass or planchette over the letters on the board. These boards are often regarded as a children's game and, indeed, started out as a Victorian pastime. They should not, however, be taken lightly, as they can disturb the minds of sensitive individuals and some children. Ouija boards can also affect the genius loci of a place. The word 'ouija' comes from the French and German words for 'Yes': 'Oui' and 'Ja'.

PARANORMAL INDUCTION

The introduction of a spirit entity to a new location by the spirit attaching itself to a person or persons and travelling with them to a new site.

PASSING CONDITIONS

Physical symptoms inflicted temporarily on a medium or psychic by a ghost entity. The conditions vary from case to case, but are normally connected with conditions experienced by the dead entity at their time of death. Passing conditions sometimes linger for a short while after the communication has ceased, before fading away.

PINPOINT LIGHTS

Dots of light often experienced at haunted locations. These are usually recorded as being seen when a ghost is trying to manifest. The lights dart around in an apparently random manner and are normally azure blue or white in colour.

PSYCHIC EPICENTRE

The point where psychic energy is most highly focused. This can be a room, an area or a physical object.

RADIOTELETHESIS

This is where a witness takes on the feelings of the ghost. This can be an emotion, a physical pain connected with the death of the ghost or the ghost's fear of the witness. It is different from clairsentience in that it is involuntary and uncontrolled.

SÉANCE

A controlled attempt to communicate with the dead, usually involving a group of persons who concentrate in a combined effort.

SPIRIT EXTRA

The term used to describe visible ghosts in photographs – used in the Victorian era when fake ghost photography was at its peak.

TABLE TILTING

The inexplicable tilting of tables, apparently of their own accord, but believed to be a form of communication from the dead. Table tilting normally takes place during a séance.

TASH/THEVSHI

Irish words for ghosts.

TELLURIC ENERGY

Energy of an unknown origin, but believed to come from the Earth. Also known as 'free energy' and 'earth energy'. Telluric is a derivative of 'tellurian', meaning 'terrestrial'.

TELLURIC ENERGY FIELD

A point at which telluric energy gathers, such as a ley-line convergence, a window area or a megalithic site (e.g. Stonehenge). A telluric energy field can span a large area from the energy centre (i.e. the standing stones, convergence point, etc.) and can be sensed by psychics at a considerable distance from the source.

TIMESLIP

A rip in the fabric of time whereby the past or future slips into the present and is experienced audibly, visually or, sometimes, physically by people from the present. Timeslips often occur on or near ley lines.

TRIGGER PERSON

A person whose very presence can induce paranormal activity.

VIGIL

Another term for a ghost hunt or investigation.

WINDOW AREA

A location where the ether is such that it may be exploited by supernatural forces to a greater extent than in other areas. Window areas can be created by uncontrolled use of a ouija board, occult ritual or black magic and, in some cases, the confluence of two or more ley lines. Buildings or locations on single ley lines can also become window areas if they are subjected to occult practices, or if extreme attention is drawn to them for their 'paranormal' interest. For example, if many people come to a building to see and discuss ghosts, then the location itself becomes a magnet for ethereal presences and may become a window area.

BIBLIOGRAPHY

500 British Ghosts & Hauntings
by Sarah Hapgood
Arthur C Clarke's World of Strange Powers
by Arthur C Clarke
Autumn Equinox by Ellen Dugan
A-Z of British Ghosts, The by Peter Underwood
Beltane by Raven Grimassi
Biography of a Ghost Hunter, The
by Harry Price
Borley Postscript by Peter Underwood
Britain's Haunted Heritage by J. A. Brooks
Candlemass by Amber K and Azrael Arynn K
Country Life, December 26th 1936
Dangerous Ghosts by Elliott O'Donnell
Encyclopaedia of Ghosts & Spirits, The
by Rosemary Ellen Guiley
End Of Borley Rectory, The by Harry Price
Enigma Of Borley Rectory, The by Ivan Banks
Field Guide to Spirit Photography
by Dale Kaczmarek
Ghost Handbook, The by John & Anne Spencer
Ghost Hunters, The by Peter Underwood
Ghost Hunter by Eddie Burks & Gillian Cribbs
Ghost Hunters The Handbook
by Peter Underwood
Ghosts & Hauntings by Dennis Bardens
Ghosts, Hauntings & The Supernatural World
by Roy Harley-Lewis
Ghosts & How to See Them
by Peter Underwood
Ghosts of Borley, The by Peter Underwood
Ghosts Of Great Britain by Jonathan Sutherland
Ghosts – The Illustrated History
by Peter Haining
Guide to Ghosts & Haunted Places
by Peter Underwood
Halloween by Silver Ravenwolf
Haunted Britain by Antony D. Hippisley Coxe
Haunted Britain by Elliott O'Donnell
Haunted Realm, The by Simon Marsden
History's Mysteries, The History Channel 2000
In Search Of Ghosts by Ian Wilson
Lancashire Magic & Mystery by Kenneth Fields
Life & Works of John Dee, The by Robert Hardy
Midsummer by Anna Franklin
Mine to Kill by David St Clair

Most Haunted House In Britain, The
by Harry Price
Nights in Haunted Houses by Peter Underwood
No Common Task by Peter Underwood
Ostara by Edain McCoy
Our Haunted Kingdom by Andrew Green
Our Haunted Lives by Jeff Belanger
Poltergeist Phenomenon, The
by John & Anne Spencer
Queen Victoria's Other World
by Peter Underwood
Scole Experiment, The by Grant Solomon
Scottish Ghost Stories by Elliott O'Donnell
Strange Magazine – 'The Haunted Boy of
Cottage City' by Mark Opsasnick
The Supernatural A-Z by James Randi
Vertical Plane, The by Ken Webster
Witchcraft Trials in Salem, The
by Douglas Linder
World's Ghost & Poltergeist Stories, The
by Sarah Hapgood
This Haunted Isle by Peter Underwood
This House is Haunted by Guy Lyon Playfair &
Maurice Grosse
Yule by Dorothy Morrisson

Websites

During my research I consulted numerous
online web resources, but the following
websites deserve particular mention:
www.occultopedia.com, www.wikipedia.com,
www.harryprice.co.uk and
ww.thescoleexperiment.com.

INDEX

AUTHOR'S ACKNOWLEDGEMENTS

I must thank New Holland's Reference Publishing Manager, Jo Hemmings, for approaching me to write this book, which has taken me on a journey into history which I have thoroughly enjoyed, and I must thank the patient Gareth Jones, Naomi Waters and Steffanie Brown, my editors, for steering me through the project without too many crashes! I am also indebted to Lionel Fanthorpe for his wonderfully exuberant foreword, and to my PA, Sian Rayner, for her hard work in conducting much of the research, spending hours in my library selecting the best historical sources of reference. I would also like to thank Dale Kaczmarek for allowing me to use his strange picture of a female spirit caught at Bachelor's Grove Cemetery, and Troy Taylor for providing a great biography. I must also mention Ian Armer, who helped me research some of the personalities mentioned in Chapter 5. Lastly I would like to thank the spirits of whatever 'other world' exists. With sightings and beliefs dating back thousands of years, there can be no doubt that we are surrounded by things which we cannot see, and I have been delighted to spend a few months flitting between this world and the next to tell their tales. May they rest in eternal peace.

PHOTOGRAPHIC CREDITS

All photographs are © TopFoto, with the exception of the following: Pages 55 & 57: © The Daily Telegraph; pages 80 & 81: © Jason Karl; page 83: © Topfoto/Fortean; © Page 86: © Ghost Research Society – used with permission; page 87(b): © Alan Palmer; page 88: © Mary Evans/Peter Underwood; page 90: © Topfoto/Fortean; pages 125 & 126: © Troy Taylor; pages 127 & 128: photos by Ian Hossack, courtesy of Peter Underwood FRSA; page 136: © Allan Marshall; pages 140 & 141: © The Scole Experimental Group; pages 142 & 143: © Leicester City Council; page 147: © Ian Addicote/www.ghosthunting.org.uk; page 149: © Historic Royal Palaces.